TAEKWON-DO PATTERNS

From Beginner to Black Belt

Master Jim Hogan

Foreword by Master Trevor Nicholls

THE CROWOOD PRESS

First published in 2006 by
The Crowood Press Ltd
Ramsbury, Marlborough
Wiltshire SN8 2HR

www.crowood.com

This impression 2018

British Library Cataloguing-in-Publication Data
A catalogue record for this book is available from the British Library.

ISBN   978 1 86126 898 3

*To my beautiful wife Patricia whose endless love and support have made my life so special
and to my darling daughter Scarlett Mae who has made my life complete. And to the memory
of my student Robert Godfrey, who provided the initial inspiration for this book.*

I would like to thank my student James Home (III Degree) for all of his time, effort and support in helping me produce this first book of its kind on ITF patterns and their applications. I would also like to thank my students Steven Walsh (III Degree) and Dean Reason (I Degree) for appearing in the applications photographs and all of the students of Hogan's Institute for their continuing support over the years. Finally I would like to thank Tim Rumble of Britannia Photographic for his artistry with the camera.

Typeset in Plantin by Bookcraft Ltd, Stroud, Gloucestershire
Printed and bound in Malaysia by Times Offset (M) Sdn Bhd

Contents

Foreword

by Master Trevor Nicholls, VIII Degree
Secretary General,
International Taekwon-Do Federation

The importance of patterns within Taekwon-Do cannot be overstated: not only do they embody core technical and aesthetic elements of Tae-Kwon-Do but they also impose a unity of purpose across the global Taekwon-Do community as they are practised and perfected by students all over the world striving to improve their understanding of this great martial art.

In writing this book, Master Hogan has made a significant contribution towards this goal by helping students to dig beneath the surface of their patterns training and to think more deeply about the self-defence applications of the movements that they are performing. Drawing on his extensive experience as a highly successful international competitor, as a renowned instructor and as a self-defence specialist, Master Hogan has produced a clear, comprehensive and, above all, practical manual that serves both as an excellent source of reference and as a thought provoking commentary on the patterns and their application.

I congratulate Master Hogan for producing this much needed work that I believe will prove invaluable to all students of Taekwon-Do, both beginners and more senior students alike.

Master Trevor Nicholls, VIII Degree

Preface

This book has been written in response to many requests from my students over the last twenty years for a manual that 'really explains' how to perform the ITF Taekwon-Do patterns (*tul*) that form the backbone of the syllabus from beginner through to black belt.

The need for this book and its approach are summed up by the phrase 'explain' as opposed to 'show'. Whilst there are many volumes that detail the moves contained in the patterns, this book seeks to go beyond mere description and to help you, the student, to better understand them and to thereby improve your performance of them. How? As well as providing move-by-move descriptions of the patterns, this book offers two additional perspectives:

Firstly and most importantly, it encourages you to consider the patterns within the core traditions of Taekwon-Do, that is, as a part of a truly practical and highly effective self-defence art. Each pattern description contains examples of possible self-defence applications for moves within the pattern. As you think more about the practical applications of the patterns, you will be able to perform them with greater realism and in turn with greater power and accuracy.

Secondly, I have drawn on decades of teaching experience to highlight common areas of difficulty as you progress through the patterns on the way to gaining your black belt. Alongside the descriptions of self-defence applications are detailed teaching tips that will help you to avoid and correct the most common mistakes made by students as you start to perform each pattern.

There is, of course, no substitute for practice and this is particularly true of learning patterns. Use this book to help you focus on the details of the patterns, practise hard to improve and become the best black belt that you can.

Master Jim Hogan, VII Degree

1 Introduction

Taekwon-Do and its Patterns

Taekwon-Do: a Modern Martial Art

Unlike many martial arts, the origins of Taekwon-Do are well documented since it was created relatively recently by General Choi Hong Hi in 1955 and spread around the world with the formation of the ITF (International Taekwon-Do Federation) in 1966. In just fifty years ITF Taekwon-Do, as defined and developed by General Choi, has grown into one of the world's most popular martial arts with an estimated eight million students including some 150,000 in the UK.

Why has Taekwon-Do become so popular? What is the major difference between Taekwon-Do and other martial arts? At a fundamental level, the answer to both questions is the same: Taekwon-Do is a truly modern martial art, specifically designed to meet the self-defence needs of all people, young or old, across diverse religions and cultures. The success of Taekwon-Do in its stated goal and the reasons why it will continue to be a developing martial art for the twenty-first century are largely explained by its core foundations.

Taekwon-Do is Based on Experience and Research
As a teenager General Choi studied Taek Kyon, a traditional Korean martial art, before travelling to Japan as a young man where he took up the study of Shotokan Karate, achieved his II Degree black belt and then returned to Korea. Although a strong and proud patriot, General Choi always acknowledged his willingness to incorporate martial arts techniques and concepts from outside Korea if he felt they could contribute. This open-minded approach continued as he developed Taekwon-Do, researching martial arts and drawing heavily on scientific principles (particularly Newtonian physics) to develop techniques that were both practical and powerful. This spirit of research and improvement continues to this day with refinements to techniques and their application being incorporated regularly into the body of Taekwon-Do knowledge.

Taekwon-Do was Initially Developed as a Military Art
Upon his return to Korea from Japan, General Choi was commissioned as an officer in the Republic of Korea army where he began teaching karate to his troops and then went on to formulate the fundamental theories and principles of Taekwon-Do. This military background not only allowed modern military tactics of attack and defence to be incorporated but also provided a uniquely realistic and experienced proving ground for the strength and effectiveness of Taekwon-Do techniques.

Taekwon-Do is Firmly Rooted in Korean Culture
Taekwon-Do was developed as a new national martial art and, on a spiritual level, draws heavily on the traditional ethical and moral principles of Korea and the wider Orient. This spiritual dimension is not religious in nature but rather focuses on traditional values such as respect for others, correct behaviour and perseverance that are shared universally, regardless of religion or culture. The Korean origin of the art is emphasized in the adoption of Korean as the lingua franca of Taekwon-Do and, of particular importance in the present context, all of the patterns represent heroic figures or events in Korean history.

It is this fusion of scientifically based research, proven effectiveness and Korean cultural background that has made Taekwon-Do the unique martial art that it is today and which the patterns embody.

The Role of Patterns in Taekwon-Do

On one level Taekwon-Do patterns (*tul*) serve a similar purpose to the pre-arranged sequences of moves practised by the student alone in many martial arts: they are a series of defensive and offensive moves against one or more imaginary opponents that are part of the core syllabus of the art. This is certainly true in Taekwon-Do where, in addition to other sparring and power demonstrations, the first nine patterns must be mastered at successive gradings before students can test for their I Degree black belts. But Taekwon-Do patterns have a role beyond being mere components of the grading syllabus and the more that you understand this the better you will be able to perform them.

Firstly, the name, number of moves and path travelled by the pattern represent aspects of Korean history and root Taekwon-Do firmly in Korean culture. Indeed the fact that there are twenty-four Taekwon-Do patterns itself symbolizes the brevity of a human life, there being twenty-four hours in a day and a whole lifetime is like a single day when compared with eternity. Similarly, each pattern is assigned a name that represents a historical figure, movement, idea or event; within a pattern further meaning may be attached to the number of moves, the diagram of the path travelled or the way the pattern starts or finishes. All of this information not only reinforces the Korean nature of Taekwon-Do but also gives you further, more subtle insight into the meaning of the patterns and how they should be performed – two good reasons for you to make sure that you learn all aspects of the meanings of the patterns.

Secondly, the patterns were created as an integral part of Taekwon-Do, a modern scientifically based self-defence art. As such they are specifically designed to introduce students to core Taekwon-Do techniques in a cumulative and progressive manner. Successive patterns not only introduce more difficult techniques in more complex combinations but also re-visit previous moves in different contexts. To get the most out of your patterns training, you should try to look at them as an integrated series of exercises rather than as 'moving on' from one pattern to the next. Try to incorporate the lessons learned in earlier patterns in each new one that you study; look out for the re-appearance of particular techniques and understand what is different in each scenario.

Thirdly (and a principle concern of this book), the patterns are designed to teach practical self-defence techniques and each and every move has practical application. Here you need to be inventive: sometimes a move or sequence of moves may have an obvious, initial application – and sometimes not. In either case you need to research the pattern by reading books such as this, talking with your instructor and fellow students, and so on, but you must also apply your own experience and imagination to dig beneath the most obvious application. There is no one application for any technique – even at the most basic level, a properly executed block can be both a defensive move to stop an attack and an offensive move to damage your opponent's attacking tool, or perhaps it is a block such as knife hand guarding block (*sonkal daebi makgi*) that can be used as an attack in its own right. Then you must consider the moves in context with each other (how does one move set up another?) and in different scenarios (what attack combinations would this sequence be effective against? How effective would it be if weapons were involved?). The more you search for and assess different applications, the more you will understand the techniques and their interactions and the better you will perform them.

Finally, the patterns pull together many different aspects of Taekwon-Do such as multiple techniques, breath control, sine wave, body shifting and so on, and, when correctly performed, should demonstrate the art in a smooth, flowing and aesthetically pleasing manner. This should be your goal in performing patterns: to understand them and to practise them so that in performing them you can show the qualities of Taekwon-Do to the best of your abilities.

How to Use This Book

The primary function of this book is to serve as a training aid for ITF Taekwon-Do students working towards their black belts. It therefore assumes that you are regularly attending classes under a qualified ITF instructor who will take you through the patterns and the rest of the ITF syllabus as your training progresses. Use this book to complement your regular training by thinking more about the patterns and their applications, better recognising your particular areas for improvement and thereby focusing your training to work on them.

Take some time to study the rest of this Introduction carefully since it will explain the layout of the book (which differs from most martial arts books on similar subjects) and how to get the best out of it.

The Structure of the Book

Chapters
The rest of this book is divided into ten further chapters. Chapter 2 covers the two sets of fundamental movements that must be performed by the beginner before starting on the patterns. Although straightforward in comparison with the more complex patterns, these fundamental movements can be regarded as the bedrock on which the patterns stand. This chapter not only details the performance of the fundamental movements themselves but also extracts from them general principles and teaching tips that apply to all patterns such as the importance of correct stances, and the use of sine wave motion to deliver power.

Chapters 3 to 11 cover each of the nine patterns learned from beginner to I Degree black belt and all share a common structure:

- An introduction to the pattern describing its main characteristics, its meaning, number of moves and diagram of the path travelled
- A move-by-move description of the pattern comprising photographs with captions for each move and certain transitions between moves running across the top half of the page
- Underneath the pattern description and on the bottom half of the page, a mixture of self-defence applications and teaching tips relating to the pattern moves shown on that page using text, photographs with captions and diagrams as appropriate.

Throughout the book, photographs are the primary method of explanation of techniques and they are divided into two distinct groups: Pattern photographs and Other photographs.

Pattern Photographs
Pattern photographs run across the top half of the page from left to right and all show the author at full height executing an individual move or at some point between moves as shown in these photographs and notes taken from pattern Chon-Ji.

Prepare to block attack from left: bring left foot parallel to right without raising body, raise hands, look left …

5 … turn 90 degrees to the left pivoting on ball of right foot, step with left leg and execute left walking stance outer forearm low section block (*gunnun so bakat palmok najunde makgi*).

6 Step forward with right walking stance middle section punch (*gunnun so kaunde ap jirugi*).

Note that photographs of distinct moves in the pattern have the number of that move in bold at the start of the caption underneath the photograph – those showing an intermediate stage have no number. Distinct moves are given their full name in English according to the following convention:

- description of the stance, e.g. 'left walking stance' (the use of 'left' and 'right' is specific to a particular stance: as a general rule, if the stance has most body weight on the back foot then that foot determines whether it is 'left' or 'right', otherwise it is determined by the front foot, e.g. 'left l-stance' means that right leg is forward but 'left walking stance' means that the left leg is forward)
- description of the attacking or blocking tool (where appropriate), e.g. 'inner forearm'
- description of the section of the body that the technique is applied to, i.e. high, middle or low
- description of the technique, e.g. 'block'.

The Korean names (in *italic*) follow the English and they conform to the same convention although 'left' and 'right' are not included.

All pattern photographs are shot full body length, three to a page, against a light background and include an orientation icon in the top left-hand corner. The orientation icon is an innovation for this book that serves a number of functions:

- all patterns start from a single point, progress in various directions and end by returning to the starting point. The path travelled is called the pattern diagram and this is the shape of the orientation icon for a given pattern.
- the performer of the pattern is represented by a solid black triangle; at the start and end of the pattern the base of the triangle is placed horizontally across the start and end point of the pattern and the apex denotes the direction that the performer is facing, i.e. towards the instructor, judges or examiners. As the pattern progresses, the triangle representing the

performer in the orientation icon is adjusted in two ways:

— by degrees of rotation to represent changes to the direction which the performer is facing
— by moving along the lines of the diagram to represent movement of the performer relative to the previous picture (note that in certain patterns where the performer must execute moves outside the path shown by the formal pattern diagram, additional dotted lines have been provided to show the actual path taken).

Not only does this simple device allow you to see instantly where a given move fits in the pattern and which direction the performer is facing, but it also allows more flexibility in the camera angle of the photograph. Rather than, for instance, always taking photographs from the perspective of the judge (opposite the performer's start position), since you know the direction the performer is facing the photograph can be taken from a different angle to give a better view of the technique.

Other Photographs

The remaining photographs are used to illustrate the general principles described in Chapter 2, pattern applications and teaching tips. All of these photographs are shot against a darker background and may vary in size and in detail depending on the context; applications and teaching tips are also clearly titled.

Study Tips

As you will have gathered, learning a new pattern involves a lot more than merely remembering the sequence of moves yet this is a necessary starting point that many students find difficult. By far the most effective approach to this exercise is to break the pattern down into sequences of moves (typically three or four) that fit together as combinations, and to work your way through these sequences in the way described.

Learn by practice

The best way to remember the moves is to fix them in your 'physical memory', by actually performing them rather than merely trying to memorize them. Even if you are running through the patterns at home or where space is limited, try to 'walk through' the moves without necessarily taking full strides or executing techniques at full range and power.

Always start from the beginning

Once you have memorized a sequence and are ready to tackle the next, always start the new sequence by running through all of the previous sequences – this will help you both to keep the previous sequences fresh in your mind as well as to appreciate the overall shape and feel of the pattern.

Learn the Korean terminology as you go

As new techniques occur in a sequence, do not progress to the next one until you have memorized the correct Korean terminology for the techniques – learning as you go will create a stronger association between the Korean terms and the techniques and make it much easier to remember them in the longer term.

Once you have memorized the moves then you can start to focus on improving your performance of the pattern. Clearly the input of your instructor and the amount that you practise are crucial here but there are a number of other factors that can help you.

Practise with realism

This is the purpose of this book – to help you to view and practise the patterns as self-defence applications. Use this book and your own imagination to construct practical applications for the moves and truly practise the patterns in the way that they were intended to be: as a series of defensive and offensive moves against imaginary opponents. Make each and every technique count: full speed, full power and right on target.

Listen to others

In addition to your instructor, try and get as much feedback as you can from your seniors and fellow students. Whilst a mirror can be a useful training aid, you can never truly 'catch yourself' – other people can spot things that you may not even be aware that you are doing. Get into the habit of asking others to watch you performing your patterns; listen to their comments and try to work on any shortcomings that they may raise.

Watch others

In the same way as you should value the feedback of others, always make a point of studying the pattern performances of other students, both senior and junior to you. Not only are you extending the same courtesy to them for watching your performance but you can learn a lot from studying others: if you spot mistakes, ask yourself if you make them too; if you see a pattern performed well, consider what made it special and how you might emulate it.

Compete

Whilst grading examinations provide a focus for your patterns practice, they will only come along at a minimum interval of three months whereas there are many competitions that you can enter. Not only do competitions give an additional focus to your training but they also provide a different kind of challenge as well as providing an opportunity to see others' performances, often of a very high standard.

The final and most important point to be made is, of course, about practice. Your progress in patterns will be directly related to the amount and quality of the practice that you undertake. As a typical student, you will almost certainly not be able to practise enough by attending classes a couple of times a week where your instructor will have to spend time on all the other aspects of Taekwon-Do as well as patterns. You must practise your patterns outside of your regular classes.

How much is enough practice? There is no correct answer – it depends on your desire to improve and the amount of time that you can devote outside of your other commitments, but you should find time to work on any new pattern that you are learning and, equally importantly, run through all of the patterns that you know on a regular basis. Whether it is once a day, once a week or once a month, set time aside to practise and improve your patterns; remember this is one of the prime purposes of patterns: to allow you to practise and develop your Taekwon-Do skills on your own. The more you practise, the more you will improve and the more you will want to improve further – a truly virtuous circle.

2 Fundamental Movements

Before starting on the patterns, the beginner must be able to perform two sets of fundamental movements, Four Direction Punch (Saju Jirugi) and Four Direction Block (Saju Makgi), as part of their first grading for 9th Gup. Although these two exercises contain few techniques and are simple for the beginner to remember, they should not be regarded as trivial since their correct execution requires knowledge of core technical aspects of Taekwon-Do that apply to all of the patterns.

Whilst this book is primarily concerned with the patterns and is not a detailed manual of how to execute Taekwon-Do techniques, there is nonetheless a key feature of Taekwon-Do that deserves special consideration before tackling the fundamental movements and patterns: that is the way you move when executing techniques and when transitioning between them. This chapter is therefore divided into three sections: an explanation of the theory and application of sine wave (*hwaldung pahdo*) motion and the performance of the two sets of fundamental movements which are used to illustrate other common features of patterns.

Sine Wave Motion in Taekwon-Do

Probably the major difference that anyone watching Taekwon-Do patterns notices when comparing them with similar exercises from other martial arts is that the Taekwon-Do practitioner moves in a different way to the others. At first glance, this difference is shown in two ways: in Taekwon-Do there is more upward and downward movement of the body and less use of hip twisting motion than in more traditional martial arts. In fact this neatly summarizes the role of sine wave (*hwaldung pahdo*) motion in Taekwon-Do: an evolving use of a downward motion of the whole body to generate maximum power and dynamic stability.

In common with many Asian martial arts (and Shotokan Karate in particular), Taekwon-Do, in its early days, emphasized the use of twisting the hip when executing techniques in order to increase the momentum of the attacking tool and thereby the power of the technique. As one of the few martial arts to include destruction testing (breaking of boards, bricks, etc with various techniques) within its core syllabus, the provable generation of maximum power has always been a key concern of Taekwon-Do and the subject of research which showed that greater power could be developed by dipping the whole body downwards at the point of impact and getting more of the body mass behind the technique than from trunk rotation alone. By combining this use of body mass with other elements of the Taekwon-Do Theory of Power and refinements such as rotating the fist in a slight backwards motion at the start of a punch to increase the momentum of the attacking tool (Taekwon-Do movements, with very few exceptions, should start with a slight backward motion), it proved possible to significantly increase the power of Taekwon-Do techniques.

However, increased power through better use of body mass is only one aspect of sine wave motion. Indeed, delivering the maximum range of up and down motion when executing a technique can be achieved by straightening the legs before dropping down into a technique; such an approach results in a saw tooth wave (*topnal pahdo*) motion as shown opposite.

Ready to step forward and punch …

… as right leg moves towards centre point, left leg straightens out raising the body to maximum height …

… before dropping down to deliver right fore fist punch in walking stance.

Whilst this motion undoubtedly delivers power, it has two major disadvantages:

- At the start of the motion the body must tense in order to begin to rise and move forward; since the body is capable of moving faster when relaxed, this initial tension slows the movement down
- The straightening out of the supporting leg in the middle of the movement produces a jerky motion that puts the body off balance which makes is harder to change direction or react to the opponent.

In order to overcome these failings and deliver the maximum power whilst keeping the body as relaxed and in balance as possible, Taekwon-Do emphasizes a sine wave motion as shown on the following page.

13

| Ready to step forward and punch … | … dip body slightly and start to rotate fist … | … step forward, raising body but not locking left leg at highest point … | … as right foot slips forward, body starts to dip down but not lean forward … | … body dips further as punch completes and right hip is thrust forward. |

Here the 'spikes' are smoothed out and the motion is performed in a much more relaxed and balanced manner due to the use of two important techniques: sine wave rhythm and knee spring.

Sine Wave Rhythm

When executing a full sine wave motion as in the stepping obverse punch above, the body must move upwards and downwards according to the following rhythm:

- **down** – from a relaxed body posture, slightly dip the body down as you start to move forward
- **up** – as the feet draw parallel to each, raise the body to its highest point
- **down** – dip the body down and into the correct stance to complete the technique.

Knee Spring

This refers to maintaining the correct degree of flexion/extension in the knee of the supporting leg as you step forward and lower, raise and lower the body between techniques. Correct, smooth bending of the knee will ensure that the body remains balanced (that is, not leaning in any direction). At no time should either knee be locked out except when required as the stance is completed; indeed, both arms and legs should always be kept slightly bent whilst the body is in motion.

Correctly executed, sine wave motion not only adds power to patterns but also helps them to 'flow', linking techniques together in a smooth, graceful rhythm. However, not all movements and transitions in the patterns are performed with a full sine wave motion (e.g. double punches) although almost all hand techniques involve raising and lowering the body to some degree – such exceptions will be highlighted in the patterns chapters.

Saju Jirugi

The exercise comprises fourteen moves in total: seven moves performed rotating in a counter-clockwise direction pivoting on the left foot and starting with a right handed punch and then repeating the moves rotating in a clockwise direction pivoting on the right foot and starting with a left handed punch.

The diagram for the pattern is:

Meaning

Saju Jirugi means Four Direction Punch.

Description

This is the first set of fundamental movements learned by the beginner and introduces the concept of turning 90 degrees to block an attack and then stepping forwards to deliver a strong counter attack.

Grading Syllabus

Beginners in Taekwon-Do wear a white belt to represent the grade of 10th Gup; white signifies innocence as that of a beginning student who has no previous knowledge of Taekwon-Do.

Saju Jirugi forms part of the grading examination for 9th Gup that is represented by a white belt with a yellow stripe.

Techniques Introduced

Stances

* parallel stance (*narani sogi*)
* walking stance (*gunnun sogi*)

Defensive

* outer forearm low section block (*bakat palmok najunde makgi*)

Offensive

* middle section obverse punch (*kaunde baro ap jirugi*)

Saju Jirugi

Ready posture:
parallel ready stance
(*narani junbi sogi*).

Prepare to punch …

1 … step forward with
right leg and execute right
walking stance middle
section punch (*gunnun
so kaunde ap jirugi*).

Teaching Tip: Obverse Punch from Parallel Stance

Ready Start as you mean to go on. Make sure that you are standing properly in the correct posture: in this case with the feet shoulder-width apart, shoulders back and relaxed, head up, looking ahead and focusing your mind on the sequence of moves that you are about to perform. All fundamental movements and patterns must start and finish at the same point.

Sine Wave Note that the sine wave motion starts in ready stance by flexing the left knee to dip the body down as the reaction (left) hand comes up and the body starts to move forward; as the left knee extends (but does not lock out) the body rises before dipping down into the right obverse punch.

Rotation To increase momentum of the attacking tool, the right fist comes slightly away and forward from the right hip as the knees start to bend at the start of the technique. As the body moves forward, the right fist is pulled back beyond the hip in a circular motion before starting to extend into the punch at the top of the sine wave motion.

Co-ordination It is essential that all of the elements of the technique finish at the same time, i.e. hands, feet and hips all stop moving and a sharp exhaling of breath takes place at the moment of impact.

Saju Jirugi

Bring right foot back half way to left foot whilst turning 90 degrees to the left pivoting on ball of left foot, preparing to block …

2 … step back with right leg and block with left walking stance outer forearm low section block (*gunnun so bakat palmok najunde makgi*).

Prepare to punch …

Teaching Tip: Outer Forearm Low Section Block

Turning Although turns should be performed as a single, flowing motion, it is helpful to think of them (regardless of degree of rotation) as two linked stages:

• Preparation: where the feet, body and hands are brought into a position and the head is looking in the direction in which the technique can be executed. Note that the body height is held at that of the previous technique, in this case dipped to the level of the obverse punch. It is critical that correct balance is maintained to avoid 'falling' into the next technique – a good way to train for this is to make sure that you can stop for a second in this position before completing the turn and technique.

• Execution: completing the turn and the next technique with a sine wave motion from the preparation position above.

Hands Avoid dropping the hands unnecessarily between techniques. In this case the right arm is already at shoulder height so when preparing to block you only need to bend the right arm and drop it slightly to the correct, solar plexus level and bring the left arm up so the fists are back to back. Similarly, as you prepare to punch after the block, raise the left arm straight up to its reaction position (held out at chest level and slightly bent) – do not drop it further and then raise it.

Saju Jirugi

3 … step forward with right walking stance middle section punch (*gunnun so kaunde ap jirugi*).

4 Bring right leg back, turn 90 degrees to the left pivoting on ball of left foot and block with left walking stance outer forearm low section block (*gunnun so bakat palmok najunde makgi*).

5 Step forward with right walking stance middle section punch (*gunnun so kaunde ap jirugi*).

Application for Outer Forearm Low Section Block: Blocking a Front Snap Kick

As attacker starts to step forward to deliver a kick, defender turns and faces preparing to block …

… as soon as attacker starts to kick, defender steps forward and blocks just above attacker's ankle joint before kick can fully extend to target.

Saju Jirugi

6 Bring right leg back, turn 90 degrees to the left pivoting on ball of left foot and block with left walking stance outer forearm low section block (*gunnun so bakat palmok najunde makgi*).

7 Step forward with right walking stance middle section punch (*gunnun so kaunde ap jirugi*).

Step with right leg to return to ready posture.

Application for Stepping Obverse Punch

As well as helping to deliver more power, extending the reaction arm can help frustrate an attack, force the opponent off balance and confuse him before …

… stepping in and executing a strong obverse punch to the middle section.

Saju Jirugi

Now movements 1–7 are repeated but this time pivoting on the right foot and turning in the opposite direction (i.e. to the right).

Only the left leg steps forward and backwards, punches are performed with the left arm and blocks with the right.

14 on the last movement – left walking stance middle section obverse punch (*gunnun so kaunde ap jirugi*) – shout '*kihap*' strongly and then 'Saju Jirugi'.

Step back with left leg to return to ready posture: parallel ready stance (*narani junbi sogi*).

General Teaching Tips

Stances The importance of correct stances cannot be overstated: correct moves cannot proceed from incorrect stances. At every stage check your stances for correct foot position, weight distribution and body attitude (full facing, half facing, and so on); use your patterns training to 'iron out' your bad habits early on.

Speed The effectiveness of techniques is dependent on their speed; the fundamental movements and patterns are designed to allow you to show your understanding of this. At the point of contact with the opponent the attacking tool must be accelerating and you should show this clearly by performing the technique at an appropriate speed (that is, starting slower than in a sparring/self-defence situation), emphasising the acceleration at the end. Exceptions to this are where the pattern dictates a particular speed, e.g. 'slow' where you emphasize the accuracy of the movement or 'fast' where you execute techniques in rapid succession.

Rhythm Fundamental movements and patterns must be performed in a rhythmic manner and not rushed through. After each technique (or sometimes two or more techniques in the patterns) try to relax your body whilst preparing for the next technique. You should not stop between techniques but there should be about a second between the end of one technique and the marked increase in acceleration of the next one.

Finishing When performing a pattern under the supervision of your instructor or seniors remember to stay in position after shouting '*kihap*' and the name of the fundamental movement or pattern and only return to the ready posture when told to do so.

Saju Makgi

The exercise comprises sixteen moves in total: eight moves performed rotating in a counter-clockwise direction pivoting on the left foot and starting with a left handed block, and then repeating the moves rotating in a clockwise direction pivoting on the right foot and starting with a right handed block.

The diagram for the pattern is:

Grading Syllabus

As with Saju Jirugi, Saju Makgi forms part of the grading examination for 9th Gup that is represented by a white belt with a yellow stripe.

Techniques Introduced

Defensive

- knife hand low section block (*sonkal najunde makgi*)
- inner forearm middle section block (*an palmok kaunde makgi*)

Meaning

Saju Makgi means Four Direction Block.

Description

This is the second set of fundamental movements learned by the beginner and introduces the concept of blocking two successive attacks to different sections of the body.

Saju Makgi

Ready posture: parallel ready stance (*narani junbi sogi*).

Prepare to block …

1 … step back with right leg and block with left walking stance knife hand low section block (*gunnun so sonkal najunde makgi*).

Teaching Tip: Hand Positions for Blocks

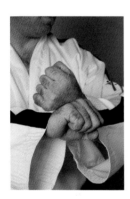

When performing outer forearm low section block (*bakat palmok najunde makgi*) or knife hand low section block (*sonkal najunde makgi*) the back of the wrist of the blocking arm is placed on top of the wrist of the reaction arm at the start of the block.

For inner forearm middle section block (*an palmok kaunde makgi*) the back of the wrist of the blocking arm is placed underneath the wrist of the reaction arm at the start of the block. Note that the reaction arm is held at the same height for both blocks.

When preparing to block and the hands are raised to solar plexus height it is important to protect the chest by keeping the hands in front of the chest (not back towards the shoulder of the reaction arm) and the elbows down so that the forearms are held at an angle of about 45 degrees.

Saju Makgi

Step forward with right leg preparing to block …

2 … with right walking stance inner forearm middle section block (*gunnun so an palmok kaunde makgi*).

Bring right foot back half way to left foot whilst turning 90 degrees to the left pivoting on ball of left foot, preparing to block …

Application for Knife Hand Low Section Block: Blocking a Front Snap Kick

Note that the attacker is closer than in the same application for Saju Jirugi since the use of the knife hand allows the defender to block the attack earlier. However, preparation for the block is the same …

… as soon as attacker starts to kick, step back and block the attacker's ankle joint before kick can fully extend to target.

Saju Makgi

3 ... step back with right leg and block with left walking stance knife hand low section block (*gunnun so sonkal najunde makgi*).

4 Step forward with right leg and block with right walking stance inner forearm middle section block (*gunnun so an palmok kaunde makgi*).

5 Bring right leg back, turn 90 degrees to the left pivoting on ball of left foot and block with left walking stance knife hand low section block (*gunnun so sonkal najunde makgi*).

Application for Knife Hand Low Section Block: Blocking a Knee Kick

As attacker prepares to kick with the knee at close quarters, defender prepares to block ...

... stepping back from knee strike and blocking with knife hand to the attacker's thigh.

The target here is the femoral artery in the attacker's thigh – executed correctly, this block will temporarily disable the attacker's leg.

Saju Makgi

6 Step forward with right leg and block with right walking stance inner forearm middle section block (*gunnun so an palmok kaunde makgi*).

7 Bring right leg back, turn 90 degrees to the left pivoting on ball of left foot and block with left walking stance knife hand low section block (*gunnun so sonkal najunde makgi*).

8 Step forward with right leg and block with right walking stance inner forearm middle section block (*gunnun so an palmok kaunde makgi*).

Application for Inner Forearm Middle Section Block: Blocking a Punch or Strike

This versatile block can be used to block a punch on the inside or outside of the attacker's arm in an inwards or outwards motion. Here the punch is blocked by attacking the inner forearm in an outwards motion.

The block is equally effective against other hand attacks. In this case it is used to block an inward knife hand strike by attacking the outer forearm in an outwards motion, making it difficult for the attacker to strike or punch again.

Saju Makgi

Now movements 1–8 are repeated but this time pivoting on the right foot and turning in the opposite direction (i.e. to the right).

Only the left leg steps forward and backwards; knife hand blocks are performed with the right hand and inner forearm blocks with the left arm.

Step with right leg to return to ready posture.

16 On the last movement – left walking stance inner forearm middle section block (*gunnun so ap palmok kaunde makgi*) – shout '*kihap*' strongly and then 'Saju Makgi'. Step back with left leg to return to ready posture: parallel ready stance (*narani junbi sogi*).

Application for Inner Forearm Middle Section Block: Attack to Arm

As opponent attempts to grab, the defender adopts the preparatory blocking position, grabbing the attacker's arm with his reaction hand …

… as defender executes the block, the attacker's arm is pulled towards the defender and the block attacks the outside of the attacker's elbow joint.

3 Chon-Ji Tul

Chon-Ji

Meaning
Chon-Ji means literally 'the Heaven the Earth'. It is, in the Orient, interpreted as the creation of the world or the beginning of human history, therefore it is the first pattern played by the beginner. This pattern consists of two similar parts, one to represent the Heaven and the other the Earth.

Description
The first of the twenty-four Taekwon-Do patterns, Chon-Ji demonstrates the foundations of good Taekwon-Do technique: powerful basic techniques and balanced movement in all directions. The pattern comprises strong hand techniques and whilst beginners enjoy being able to show the strength of their punches and blocks, this strength can tend to be over-emphasized as the subtlety of Taekwon-Do techniques takes time to learn. Try to show not only accurate, powerful techniques but also good balance, co-ordination and sine wave.

There are nineteen moves in the pattern: eight in the first part and eleven in the second. The diagram for the pattern is:

Grading Syllabus
Chon-Ji is taught at 9th Gup and forms part of the grading examination for 8th Gup that is represented by a yellow belt. Yellow signifies the Earth from which a plant sprouts and takes root as the Taekwon-Do foundation is being laid.

Techniques Introduced

Stances

- l-stance (*niunja sogi*)

Chon-Ji

Ready posture: parallel ready stance (*narani junbi sogi*).

Prepare to block attack from left: dip body, look left and raise hands ...

1 ... turn 90 degrees to the left pivoting on ball of right foot, step with left leg and execute left walking stance outer forearm low section block (*gunnun so bakat palmok najunde makgi*).

Teaching Tip: Preparing to Block

All but two of the coloured belt patterns start by stepping in from an upright ready position with a block against an attack from the side, and whilst this is not a move in itself it nonetheless deserves detailed study and practice. Correct execution of this preparatory technique will not only get your patterns off to a good start but will also stand you in good stead for a common yet difficult self defence scenario where you are aware of a possible attack in the corner of your field of vision or outside of it and you must react immediately without being certain of the nature of the attack. By preparing to block correctly as shown in the picture above, you achieve three immediate advantages:

You are ready to move With your head turned towards the attacker you can now see the situation clearly and you must move either towards or away from the attacker before the attack is completed.

Whatever your decision, with your knees bent and your weight slightly more on the back foot, you are in the optimal position to move as fast as possible in any direction.

You are ready to block Your hands are in position to execute a range of blocks or perhaps deliver a knife hand strike. Note that the hands come straight up to this position and are held at about eighteen inches (40cm) from the body at solar plexus height in order to deliver the technique with maximum power.

You are protected Your side facing posture offers the smallest target to the attacker; note carefully the position of the elbows: they are not held high but allowed to drop to their natural, relaxed position with the forearms at an angle of about 45 degrees which helps protect the side of the ribcage.

Chon-Ji

Prepare to punch …

2 … step forward with right walking stance middle section punch (*gunnun so kaunde ap jirugi*).

Begin to draw back right leg at start of turning 180 degrees to the right, maintaining same height as in previous move, not dropping right arm and starting to raise left.

Teaching Tip: Walking Stance

One of the first stances learned by the beginner, this strong stance emphasizes the power generated by using the sine wave motion and is the bedrock for much of Taekwon-Do patterns and drilling. Try hard to perfect moving in this stance early in your Taekwon-Do training as faults left uncorrected are difficult to rectify later on. The most common areas of difficulty for beginners are as follows.

Width Whilst beginners are aware of the dimensions of the walking stance (one shoulder width wide and one and a half shoulder widths long) and will start with the correct width, as the pattern progresses the stance will frequently become narrower. The primary reason for this is lack of concentration as the beginner is focused on remembering the moves and 'getting through it'. Slow down; the stance is equally as important as the technique that is executed in it. Make a conscious effort to try to plant your leading foot the correct distance from your back foot, particularly when turning, where the leading foot must

be placed one shoulder width from the inside of the back foot rather than just straight ahead.

Locking out the back leg When stepping into walking stance it is essential that you lock out the back leg at the exact moment that the technique is executed and the stance completed – this action gives the stance strength and adds to the power of the technique. Again, failure to do so is often a symptom of rushing through the pattern – do not start the next move until the current one is fully completed.

Weight distribution Remember, your body weight must be distributed equally between both legs while adhering to the dimensions of the stance; in trying to emphasize the power of their techniques beginners often bend the knee of the leading leg too much, shifting their body weight forward from the centre. Make sure that you can see all of your leading foot when you look down and that it is not partially obscured by your knee.

Chon-Ji

… without raising body bring right foot parallel to left, pivot on ball of left foot to face forward, position hands ready to block and look right …

3 … complete turn, step forward with right walking stance outer forearm low section block (*gunnun so bakat palmok najunde makgi*).

4 Step forward with left walking stance middle section punch (*gunnun so kaunde ap jirugi*).

Application for Outer Forearm Low Section Block: Sweeping a Front Snap Kick

As well as using the block to stop the kick, it can also be modified to continue travelling at the point of impact, delivering the final twist six inches (15cm) or so later. This sweeps the attacker's leg to the side, putting him off balance and vulnerable to a counter attack.

If the attacker kicks with the other leg then the same sweep can be generated by executing the block to the outside of the attacking leg.

Chon-Ji

Prepare to block attack from left: bring left foot parallel to right without raising body, raise hands, look left …

5 … turn 90 degrees to the left pivoting on ball of right foot, step with left leg and execute left walking stance outer forearm low section block (*gunnun so bakat palmok najunde makgi*).

6 Step forward with right walking stance middle section punch (*gunnun so kaunde ap jirugi*).

Application for Turn and Block: Defending Against a Second Rushing Attacker

Having counter attacked first attacker with a middle section punch, a second attacker rushes in from the side …

… defender turns and delivers low section block to second attackers lead leg at close quarters aiming for the femoral artery …

… following up with a middle section reverse punch.

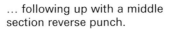

31

Chon-Ji

7 Bring right foot parallel to left foot, turn 180 degrees to the right pivoting on ball of left foot and block with right walking stance outer forearm low section block (*gunnun so bakat palmok najunde makgi*).

8 Step forward with left walking stance middle section punch (*gunnun so kaunde ap jirugi*).

Prepare to block attack from left: bring left foot parallel to right, raise hands (left hand underneath, palm facing down), look left …

Teaching Tip: L-Stance

Whilst the walking stance allows full commitment of your whole body weight to a technique, the l-stance offers a compromise between less total commitment and a good defensive posture along with easier movement of the body both forwards and backwards. As such, it is used as the main stance in sparring drills since it combines a more cautious, half facing posture with the ability to move and launch an attack rapidly, particularly with the front foot, due to the weight being largely on the back foot. Some key points to watch out for include:

Weight distribution Remember that 70 per cent of the weight is on the back foot and for beginners this is frequently more than they think. A useful test is that in l-stance you should be able to avoid an attempt to sweep the lead leg by simply raising it or moving it backwards without any change in your balance, so if you find yourself leaning backwards to maintain balance when you raise your lead leg off the floor then you have got too much weight on the front leg and if you need to lean forwards then you have too much weight on the back leg.

Position of rear leg The rear leg must be sufficiently bent so that the heel and hip are in a straight vertical line with the knee above the foot; resist the temptation to straighten the back leg: to maintain this position takes effort and your legs should feel tired after time spent in l-stance.

Stepping When stepping in l-stance you must ensure that you pivot on the ball of your lead foot when stepping forwards and your rear foot when stepping backwards. To help you achieve this when stepping forwards turn the lead foot out by about 15 degrees before starting to step.

Chon-Ji

9 ... turn 90 degrees to the left pivoting on ball of right foot, step into right I-stance inner forearm middle section block (*niunja so an palmok kaunde makgi*).

10 Step forward with right walking stance middle section punch (*gunnun so kaunde ap jirugi*).

11 Bring right foot parallel left foot, turn 180 degrees to the right pivoting on ball left foot and block with left I-stance inner forearm middle section block (*niunja so an palmok kaunde makgi*).

Application for 180-degree Turn and Block: Release from a Grab from Behind

The act of turning can be used to help release from a grab as in this situation where the attacker grabs the defender's shoulders from behind ...

... as the defender turns, the attacker's grip is weakened ...

... and broken with a high section inner forearm block.

Chon-Ji

12 Step forward with left walking stance middle section punch (*gunnun so kaunde ap jirugi*).

13 Turn 90 degrees to the left pivoting on ball of right foot, step forward with right I-stance inner forearm middle section block (*niunja so an palmok kaunde makgi*).

14 Step forward with right walking stance middle section punch (*gunnun so kaunde ap jirugi*).

Application for Inner Forearm Block: Attack to Ribcage

As opponent attempts to grab, the defender adopts the preparatory blocking position, grabbing the attacker's arm with his reaction hand …

… as defender executes the block, the attacker's arm is pulled towards the defender and the block strikes the attacker's ribcage.

Chon-Ji

15 Turn 180 degrees to the right pivoting on ball of left foot, step into left l-stance inner forearm middle section block (*niunja so an palmok kaunde makgi*).

16 Step forward with left walking stance middle section punch (*gunnun so kaunde ap jirugi*).

17 Step forward with right walking stance middle section punch (*gunnun so kaunde ap jirugi*).

Application for Stepping Forward and Punching: Pursuing a Counter Attack

When the first counter attack is not delivered with sufficient power, is off target or the attacker starts to move out of range …

… and it throws the attacker off balance in a backwards direction …

… pursuing the attacker with a second punch may finally dissuade him.

Chon-Ji

18 Step backwards with right leg and execute left walking stance middle section punch (*gunnun so kaunde ap jirugi*).

19 Step backwards with left leg, execute right walking stance middle section punch (*gunnun so kaunde ap jirugi*) and shout *'kihap'* and then 'Chon-Ji'.

Step forward with left leg to return to ready posture: parallel ready stance (*narani junbi sogi*).

Application for Stepping Back and Punching: Defence Against Rushing Attack

As attacker rushes in and is too close to step forward with counter attack, defender starts to step back and prepares to punch ...

... executing punch as attacker continues to move forward, using his momentum against him to deliver a powerful blow.

4 Dan-Gun Tul

Dan-Gun

Meaning
Dan-Gun is named after the holy Dan Gun, the legendary founder of Korea in the year 2333BC.

Description
Building on the basic punching and blocking of Chon-Ji, this fast, powerful pattern points the student in two new directions that reveal the diversity and range of Taekwon-Do techniques.

First, an alternative attacking tool is introduced with the knife hand side strike (*sonkal yop taerigi*). A key feature of Taekwon-Do is its many varied attacking (and blocking) tools and techniques, their appropriate targets and circumstances for their use. As each new technique is introduced (and the patterns introduce a great number of them), try to discover its unique qualities and this will help you in identifying effective applications.

Second, in addition to the sheer number of techniques, the idea of linking them together in different ways is now introduced with the concept of 'continuous motion' (two techniques executed within a single breath); further differing 'motions' are introduced in later patterns.

There are twenty-one moves in the pattern and its diagram is:

Grading Syllabus
Dan-Gun is taught at 8th Gup and forms part of the grading examination for 7th Gup that is represented by a yellow belt with a green stripe.

Techniques Introduced

Defensive

- knife hand middle section guarding block (*sonkal kaunde daebi makgi*)
- twin forearm block (*sang palmok makgi*)
- outer forearm rising block (*bakat palmok choo-kyo makgi*)

Offensive

- high section obverse punch (*nopunde baro ap jirugi*)
- knife hand side strike (*sonkal yop taerigi*)

Dan-Gun

Ready posture: parallel ready stance (*narani junbi sogi*).

Prepare to block attack from left: dip body, look left and raise hands with right hand higher than left, left palm facing towards you and right facing away …

1 … turn 90 degrees to the left, step with left leg into right I-stance knife hand middle section guarding block (*niunja so sonkal kaunde daebi makgi*).

Application for Knife Hand Guarding Block: Blocking a Punch and Defensive Posture

Guarding blocks combine effective close quarter blocking with an excellent defensive posture. Here a middle section punch is blocked using knife hand guarding block against the inside of the attacker's arm …

… and it is equally effective against the outside of the attacker's arm. In both cases the defender seeks to attack the wrist joint with a breaking technique.

Note how the side facing posture of the I-stance reduces the body area vulnerable to a frontal attack while the elbow of the lead arm protects the ribs and the other hand protects the solar plexus.

Dan-Gun

Prepare to punch …

2 … step forward with right walking stance high section punch (*gunnun so nopunde ap jirugi*).

Prepare to turn 180 degrees to the right by pivoting on ball of left foot, without raising body bring right foot parallel to left, raise hands and look right …

Teaching Tip: High, Middle and Low Section Techniques

The height of an attack (or block) is relative to the attacker's (or defender's) own body. When the attacking tool reaches the attacker's eye level at the point of impact, it is termed a high section attack as in the punch above.

A middle section attack is when the attacking tool reaches the attacker's shoulder level at the point of impact. Thus the actual point of impact is a function of the section aimed at and the relative heights of attacker and defender …

… as in this low section punch when the attacking tool reaches the attacker's lower abdomen at the point of impact, although the target in this case is the face since the defender is kneeling.

Dan-Gun

3 ... complete turn, step forward with right leg into left I-stance knife hand middle section guarding block (*niunja so sonkal kaunde daebi makgi*).

4 Step forward with left walking stance high section punch (*gunnun so nopunde ap jirugi*).

Prepare to block attack from left: bring left foot parallel to right without raising body, raise hands, look left ...

Application for Knife Hand Guarding Block: Blocking a Side Kick

As attacker raises leading leg for side kick, defender raises hands and prepares to push off the front foot and slide ...

... back into knife hand guarding block, blocking the kick with the lead hand, targeting the attacker's Achilles tendon of the kicking leg.

Dan-Gun

5 ... turn 90 degrees to the left pivoting on ball of right foot, step with left leg and execute left walking stance outer forearm low section block (*gunnun so bakat palmok najunde makgi*).

6 Step forward with right walking stance high section punch (*gunnun so nopunde ap jirugi*).

7 Step forward with left walking stance high section punch (*gunnun so nopunde ap jirugi*).

Application for Outer Forearm Block and Stepping Punch: Blocking a Front Snap Kick and Counter Attacking

As attacker launches a front snap kick, defender steps in with a strong outer forearm low section block ...

... causing attacker to fall away from defender who steps forward to ...

... counter attack with high section obverse punch.

Dan-Gun

8 Step forward with right walking stance high section punch (*gunnun so nopunde ap jirugi*).

Turning 270 degrees to the left, pivot on ball of right foot without raising body to face the opposite direction, bring left foot parallel to right and raise hands with palms facing inwards and right hand underneath, look to the left …

9 … step with left foot and into right I-stance twin forearm block (*niunja so sang palmok makgi*).

Application for Twin Forearm Block: Defence Against Two Simultaneous Attacks

Two attackers close in, one from the front to throw a punch to the defender's middle section and one from the side to strike downwards onto the defender's head/shoulder.

Defender executes twin forearm block blocking the punch with outer forearm middle section block and the downward strike with outer forearm rising block.

Dan-Gun

10 Step forward with right leg and execute right walking stance high section punch (*gunnun so nopunde ap jirugi*).

Prepare to turn 180 degrees to the right by pivoting on ball of left foot, without raising body bring right foot parallel to left, raise hands and look right …

11 … step with right foot and into left I-stance twin forearm block (*niunja so sang palmok makgi*).

Application for Twin Forearm Block: Defence and Counter Attack Against High Hooking Punch

As attacker prepares to throw a high section hooking punch, defender raises hands and …

… executes twin forearm block, blocking hooking punch with rising block and simultaneously counter attacking with forearm strike to attacker's chest.

Dan-Gun

12 Step forward with left walking stance high section punch (*gunnun so nopunde ap jirugi*).

13 Turn 90 degrees to left pivoting on ball of right foot and step forward with left walking stance outer forearm low section block (*gunnun so bakat palmok najunde makgi*) and …

14 … immediately execute left walking stance outer forearm rising block (*gunnun so bakat palmok chookyo makgi*). Moves 13 and 14 are performed as a continuous motion.

Teaching Tip: Continuous Motion

Throughout the patterns there are sets of moves that are required to be performed as particular 'motions' outside of the normal rhythm of the patterns. In this case, two blocks, outer forearm low section block (*bakat palmok najunde makgi*) and outer forearm rising block (*bakat palmok chookyo makgi*) must be performed from the same stance using the same attacking tool as a 'continuous motion' which seeks to highlight how two separate movements can be linked together smoothly, adding to the grace and beauty of the pattern.

All calls for continuous motion in the coloured belt patterns (in Dan-Gun and later in Toi-Gye) require two separate techniques to be performed as follows.

- There should be no 'gap' between techniques – as soon as one finishes the other begins: that is not to say that they are rushed or performed at ab-

normal speed, merely that one flows directly from the other.

- Each technique must be performed with a full, 'down-up-down', i.e. immediately after the first low section block with the rear leg locked, the body must dip down slightly further by bending the knee and raising the heel a little as you start the rising block.
- To further demonstrate the linking of the techniques, control your breathing so that you breathe in at the start of the first technique and breathe out continuously during both techniques emphasising the exhalation at the end of each technique.
- In this case, remember to show clearly that the first technique is performed with the body in a half-facing posture and the second in a full-facing posture.

Dan-Gun

15 Step forward with right leg into right walking stance outer forearm rising block (*gunnun so bakat palmok chookyo makgi*).

16 Step forward with left leg into left walking stance outer forearm rising block (*gunnun so bakat palmok chookyo makgi*).

17 Step forward with right leg into right walking stance outer forearm rising block (*gunnun so bakat palmok chookyo makgi*).

Application for Rising Block: Defence and Counter Attack against High Section Punch

Rising block is highly effective against a high section punch with the blocking forearm striking the attacker's radial nerve causing a degree of temporary disablement …

… which allows the defender to grab the attacking fist from underneath with his reaction hand …

… and twist the attacker's arm so that the attacker's elbow joint can be locked against the defender's blocking arm.

Dan-Gun

Turn 270 degrees to the left pivoting on ball of right foot without raising body to face the opposite direction, bring left foot parallel to right, raise hands and look to the left …

18 … complete turn and step with left leg into right I-stance knife hand side strike (*niunja so sonkal yop taerigi*).

19 Step forward with right walking stance high section punch (*gunnun so nopunde ap jirugi*).

Application for Knife Hand Strike: Attack to the Throat

As attacker rushes in from the side and slightly behind, the defender …

… intercepts attacker with side strike to the throat area.

Dan-Gun

20 Turn 180 degrees to the right and execute left I-stance knife hand side strike (*niunja so sonkal yop taerigi*).

21 Step forward with left walking stance high section punch (*gunnun so nopunde ap jirugi*), shout '*kihap*' and then 'Dan-Gun'.

Step back with left leg and return to ready posture: parallel ready stance (*narani junbi sogi*).

Application for 180-degree Turn and Knife Hand Strike: Release from a Grab and Counter Attack

Attacker grabs defender's shoulders from behind …

… as defender half turns and breaks grip, grabbing attacker's hand with his reaction arm …

… and pulling the attacker onto a knife hand strike to the ribcage.

5 Do-San Tul

Do-San

Meaning

Do-San is the pseudonym of the patriot Ahn Chang-Ho (1876–1938). The twenty-four movements represent his entire life which he devoted to furthering education in Korea and to its independence movement.

Description

Do-San develops the notion of techniques flowing together by introducing more complex combinations of techniques such as executing a fingertip thrust, having your hand grabbed and breaking the grab with a circular movement that ends in a counter attack (movements 6 and 7).

Among the new techniques introduced in Do-San is the first kick in the patterns, the front snap kick. Taekwon-Do is justifiably famous for its vast repertoire of spectacular kicks and, for the beginner, Do-San marks the point at which they start to use the whole range of attacking tools and techniques as they progress through the grades. Remember that both relatively simple kicks such as the front snap kick and more complex ones such as jumping and multiple kicks must be executed with the same speed, accuracy, power and balance as hand techniques: this requires a lot of training but to switch easily between using your legs and hands is central to your progress in Taekwon-Do.

There are twenty-four moves in the pattern and its diagram is:

Grading Syllabus

Do-San is taught at 7th Gup and forms part of the grading examination for 6th Gup that is represented by a green belt. Green signifies the plant's growth as the Taekwon-Do skill begins to develop.

Techniques Introduced

Stances
- sitting stance (*annun sogi*)

Defensive
- outer forearm high section side block (*bakat palmok nopunde yop makgi*)
- outer forearm high section wedging block (*bakat palmok nopunde hechyo makgi*)

Offensive
- straight fingertip thrust (*sun sonkut tulgi*)
- back fist high section side strike (*dung joomuk nopunde yop taerigi*)
- middle section front snap kick (*kaunde apcha busigi*)

Do-San

Ready posture: parallel ready stance (*narani junbi sogi*).

1 Turn 90 degrees to the left and step with left leg to block attack with left walking stance outer forearm high section side block (*gunnun so bakat palmok nopunde yop makgi*).

Prepare to counter punch by lowering left arm to shoulder height, raising body upwards and forwards by coming up on the ball of the right foot to deliver …

Application for Outer Forearm High Section Side Block: Blocking a High Section Punch

This block can be used to defend against straight punches to the head, attacking either the inside or, as above, the outside of the attacking tool targeting the wrist.

Here the block is used against a high hook punch by stepping in at an angle to the attacker and blocking the inside of the attacking tool targeting the elbow joint.

Do-San

2 ... left walking stance middle section reverse punch (*gunnun so kaunde bandae jirugi*) forcing the right heel back to the floor at the moment of impact.

Prepare to execute a spot turn to the right: without raising body or dropping hands move left foot half a shoulder width to the right, raise hands ready for blocking, slip right foot back and look to the right ...

3 ... pivoting on ball of left foot step forward with right foot to complete 180 degrees turn with right walking stance outer forearm high section side block (*gunnun so bakat palmok nopunde yop makgi*).

Application for Standing Reverse Punch: Rapid Counter Attack

Having blocked attacker's high section punch with an outer forearm block ...

... coming up on the ball of foot of the back leg allows the defender to generate a full sine wave ...

... and rapidly deliver a strong reverse punch counter attack without moving from his current position.

Do-San

4 Counter attack with right walking stance middle section reverse punch (*gunnun so kaunde bandae jirugi*).

5 Bring right foot parallel to left, pivot on ball of left foot, turn 90 degrees to the left and step forward with left leg into right I-stance knife hand middle section guarding block (*niunja so sonkal kaunde daebi makgi*).

As you start to step forward with right leg to counter attack, hold fists at shoulder height with elbows protecting chest …

Application for 90-degree Turn and Knife Hand Guarding Block: Evasion and Counter Attack against Front Snap Kick from Side

As attacker steps in from the side and starts to raise rear leg to kick …

… defender evades front snap kick by bringing rear leg to front leg, turning 90 degrees and …

… counter attacking by stepping forward with knife hand guarding block using the lead hand to strike the attacker's collar bone.

Do-San

6 … and step into right walking stance middle section straight fingertip thrust (*gunnun so kaunde sun sonkut tulgi*).

Release from grab by twisting the attacking hand and body to the left until palm faces downward, bending knees and coming up on the balls of the feet …

… continue to turn to the left by pivoting on ball of right foot and crossing forearms with left underneath right and both palms facing away …

Application for Straight Fingertip Thrust and Release: Counter Attack then Release and Counter a Grab

Defender counter attacks with straight fingertip thrust to attacker's solar plexus …

… but attacker recovers from counter attack and grabs defender's hand …

… defender twists away to release grab whilst thrusting released hand forward and counter attacking to opponent's groin.

Do-San

7 ... complete 360 degrees turn by stepping forward with left leg and left walking stance back fist high section side strike (*gunnun so dung joomuk nopunde yop taerigi*).

8 Step forward with right leg and right forearm crossed under left into right walking stance back fist high section side strike (*gunnun so dung joomuk nopunde yop taerigi*).

9 Pivot on the ball of right foot to turn 270 degrees to the left, step forward with left leg and block with left walking stance outer forearm high section side block (*gunnun so bakat palmok nopunde yop makgi*).

Application for Back Fist Side Strike: Evade Side Kick and Counter Attack

Here, the defender evades the attacker's side kick by drawing back his leading leg and ...

... stepping in with back fist side strike to the opponent's temple; note that the attacking arm is slightly bent and wrist is also slightly bent backwards to allow the back fist to make proper contact with the target.

Do-San

10 Counter attack with left walking stance middle section reverse punch (*gunnun so kaunde bandae jirugi*).

11 Spot turn 180 degrees to the right pivoting on ball of left foot and block with right walking stance outer forearm high section side block (*gunnun so bakat palmok nopunde yop makgi*).

12 Counter attack with right walking stance middle section reverse punch (*gunnun so kaunde bandae jirugi*).

Application for Outer Forearm High Section Block: Release from Choke

Attacker grabs defender by the throat with a straight arm – defender raises hands, turns slightly to the side …

… and turns back rapidly with a strong block to the elbow joint of the attacking arm which releases the choke.

Do-San

Pivot on ball of right foot to turn 135 degrees to the left, crossing forearms with palms facing face and left on top drawing left foot back towards right and then …

13 … step forward with left leg and block with left walking stance outer forearm high section wedging block (*gunnun so bakat palmok nopunde hechyo makgi*).

14 Keep the arms in place and counter attack with right middle section front snap kick (*kaunde apcha busigi*).

Application for Wedging Block: Blocking a Twin Vertical Punch/Breaking a Shoulder Grab

The primary purpose of the wedging block is to defend against two-handed attacks such as the twin vertical punch. As the attacker raises both hands and steps in with twin vertical punch to the face, the defender steps back and blocks with wedging block attacking the inside of the attacker's forearms.

It is also highly effective in breaking a high section grab as above where the attacker grabs defender's arms just below the shoulders, defender crosses arms and brings them up sharply between attacker's arms …

… and breaks the grab with a strong wedging block.

55

Do-San

As you retract the kicking leg, extend the left arm and place the right fist on the right hip to prepare to …

15 … step forward with the right leg and continue to counter attack with right walking stance middle section punch (*gunnun so kaunde ap jirugi*). Note that you deliver the punch with the left heel raised …

16 … in order to force the heel down as you immediately deliver right walking stance middle section reverse punch (*gunnun so kaunde bandae jirugi*). Moves 15 and 16 are performed as a fast motion.

Teaching Tip: Fast Motion

Following on from the concept of continuous motion in pattern Dan-Gun, 'fast' motion also links two or more, generally attacking, techniques together but in a more urgent and aggressive manner. In some cases this may mean simply executing the techniques in rapid succession (as in pattern Hwa-Rang moves 18 and 19, two stepping turning kicks) but in this case and others involving obverse and reverse punches after a front snap kick they must be performed as follows.

- As in continuous motion, there should be no pause between techniques – as soon as the obverse punch is completed, the reverse punch must begin.

- In order to speed up the techniques, it is necessary to modify the sine wave such that the two techniques 'share' the same sine wave, i.e. you are already 'up' as the first technique is executed and then drop 'down' into the second. This means that your body is slightly further forward than usual as you execute the obverse punch with your heel raised, reverting to its normal distance from the target when dropping down into the reverse punch.

- Each technique is performed with a full breath exhaling completely as you complete the obverse punch and inhaling and exhaling for the reverse punch.

Do-San

17 Pivot on ball of left foot to turn 90 degrees to the right and step forward (preparing with right hand on top of left) with right leg into right walking stance outer forearm high section wedging block (*gunnun so bakat palmok nopunde hechyo makgi*).

18 Keep the arms in place and counter attack with left middle section front snap kick (*kaunde apcha busigi*).

19 After preparing to punch by extending the right arm, step forward raising right heel with left walking stance middle section punch (*gunnun so kaunde ap jirugi*).

Teaching Tip: Front Snap Kick

This fast kick (usually to the low or middle sections) starts with the knee of the kicking leg brought sharply up to the height of the kick, in this case parallel to the floor for a middle section kick.

Execute the kick by extending the leg in a fast snapping motion with the toes pulled back, the hips pushed slightly forward and the supporting leg slightly bent to deliver maximum power.

After delivering the kick, pull the kicking leg back sharply into the starting position to avoid the leg being grabbed and to be ready to deliver another kick or technique.

Do-San

20 As in move 16, force the heel down as you deliver left walking stance middle section reverse punch (*gunnun so kaunde bandae jirugi*). Moves 19 and 20 are performed as a fast motion.

21 Withdraw left foot slightly, pivot on right heel, turn 45 degrees to the left and step with left leg into left walking stance forearm rising block (*gunnun so bakat palmok chookyo makgi*).

22 Step forward with right leg into right walking stance forearm rising block (*gunnun so bakat palmok chookyo makgi*).

Application for Forearm Rising Block: Blocking an Overhead Strike with Weapon

As attacker prepares to strike downwards with a weapon to the top of the defender's head, the defender prepares to step in and block. Note that with a long weapon such as the stick above, the closer the defender can block to the attacker's hands, the less force he will need to absorb from the weapon in the block.

Defender blocks weapon with front rising block as early in the striking motion as possible. Note that the blocking arm is held at 45 degrees better to absorb the striking force and deflect the striking tool away from the head.

Do-San

Pivot on ball of right foot to turn 180 degrees to the left keeping knees bent, raise hands back to back with right on top and look left in preparation for knife hand side strike … .

… as you begin the technique, the left foot traces an arc on the floor …

23 … before coming back onto pattern line with left sitting stance knife hand side strike (*annun so sonkal yop taerigi*).

Teaching Tip: Sitting Stance

The purpose of this stance is to provide the same strength and stability as a rider astride a horse and in the same manner it is not a 'passive' stance but requires continuous effort when being performed. Perhaps this is one of the reasons why beginners often have difficulty with the sitting stance and frequently seem to settle for an easier 'compromise' but it is worth perfecting not only because it will make your patterns so much better but also because it will help to develop the muscles in your legs in the process. Try to incorporate the following points in your training:

Width Having the correct width (one and a half shoulder widths between the big toes) is absolutely crucial and rarely seen in the beginner – it is well worth measuring the correct distance with a piece of string and correcting your stance accordingly.

Posture Your body must be erect with your head up, back straight, chest out and hips pulled into line tensing the abdomen.

Legs The feet must point forward with the knees bent and pushed out sufficiently for you to feel the outer edges of your feet pushing into the floor – this (for non-horse riders) is not a natural position and requires you to tense your inner thighs to achieve it. If you are performing the stance correctly then your thighs will quickly start to tire; resist the temptation to take the pressure off your thighs by straightening your legs: in fact, at no time should your legs be fully straightened either when executing a technique or moving between sitting stances.

Movement When moving laterally into and between sitting stances remember to describe a small arc on the ground with the leading foot.

Do-San

Prepare for right knife hand side strike by moving left foot in arc back to right foot, keeping knees bent, hands raised with right on top and looking right, then …

24 … move right foot in arc and into right sitting stance knife hand side strike (*annun so sonkal yop taerigi*), shout '*kihap*' and then 'Do-San'.

Step with right leg and return to ready posture: parallel ready stance (*narani junbi sogi*).

Application for Knife Hand Side Strike: Counter Attack to Ribcage

As attacker steps forward with a punch, defender draws back to evade technique and raises hands in preparation for …

… knife hand side strike to attacker's ribcage. Note that by stepping with an arc into sitting stance, defender has stepped past attacker's leading leg and is in range for the strike.

6   Won-Hyo Tul

Won-Hyo

Meaning
Won-Hyo was the noted monk who introduced Buddhism to the Silla Dynasty in the year 686AD.

Description
As the student progresses new techniques and combinations are introduced at a faster pace and this is certainly the case in Won-Hyo with new stances, kicks, punches, strikes and blocks put together in longer, flowing combinations. Pay particular attention to the combination at the start of the pattern (movements 1, 2 and 3) which links a twin forearm block with an inward knife hand strike and side punch as counter attacks: this close quarters sequence requires flowing sine wave and a subtle stance change to make maximum power delivery possible.

The side piercing kick makes its first appearance in Won-Hyo – a very powerful technique that requires flexibility in the hips and good co-ordination of hands and feet. To emphasize your mastery of this challenging kick, try to kick at the top of the target area, i.e. kick at shoulder height when kicking middle section.

There are twenty-eight moves in the pattern and its diagram is:

Grading Syllabus
Won-Hyo is taught at 6th Gup and forms part of the grading examination for 5th Gup that is represented by a green belt with a blue stripe.

Techniques Introduced

Stances
- close ready stance A (*moa junbi sogi A*)
- fixed stance (*gojung sogi*)
- bending ready stance (*guburyo junbi sogi*)

Defensive
- inner forearm middle section circular block (*an palmok kaunde dollimyo makgi*)
- forearm middle section guarding block (*palmok kaunde daebi makgi*)

Offensive
- knife hand high section inward strike (*sonkal nopunde anuro taerigi*)
- middle section side punch (*kaunde yop jirugi*)
- middle section side piercing kick (*kaunde yopcha jirugi*)
- low section front snap kick (*najunde apcha busigi*)

61

Won-Hyo

Ready posture: close ready stance A (*moa junbi sogi A*).

1 Dip body, look left, raise hands with left hand underneath and palms facing you; turn 90 degrees to the left and step with left foot into right I-stance twin forearm block (*niunja so sang palmok makgi*).

Raise body without quite straightening legs and extend arms away from body in preparation for …

Teaching Tip: Close Ready Stances

There are three close stances in the coloured belt patterns; all are based on standing erect with the feet together and differ in the position of the arms.

In type A the left hand covers the right fist held at a distance of 30cm from the philtrum with the elbows held at the natural height.

In type B the left hand also covers the right fist but it is held at a distance of 15cm from the navel.

In type C the left palm covers the right with the left middle finger on top of the right and held at a distance of 10cm from the lower abdomen.

Won-Hyo

2 … dropping down into right I-stance knife hand high section inward strike (*niunja so sonkal nopunde anuro taerigi*). Note that the left reaction arm is pulled back to just below the right shoulder.

Pull back left foot, extend right hand and pull left fist back to left hip before …

3 … slipping the left foot into left fixed stance middle section side punch (*gojung so kaunde yop jirugi*).

Application for Knife Hand Inward Strike: Release from Choke

Attacker grabs defender by throat, defender raises hands …

… and attacks elbow of attacker's arm with inward knife hand strike.

Won-Hyo

Bring left foot to right, prepare hands for twin forearm block with right hand underneath and turn 180 degrees to the right pivoting on the ball of the left foot …

4 … and step forward with right foot into left I-stance twin forearm block (*niunja so sang palmok makgi*).

5 Raise the body and the drop down into left I-stance knife hand high section inward strike (*niunja so sonkal nopunde anuro taerigi*).

Application for Knife Hand Inward Strike: Pulling Opponent onto Neck Strike

Having blocked the attacker's punch, the defender grabs the attacker's sleeve with his blocking hand …

… and pulls the attacker onto a knife hand high section inward strike targeting the carotid artery.

Won-Hyo

6 Slip the right foot forwards and execute right fixed stance middle section side punch (*gojung so kaunde yop jirugi*).

7 Move right foot to left, turning 90 degrees to the right and into right bending ready stance (*guburyo junbi sogi*).

8 Execute left middle section side piercing kick (*kaunde yopcha jirugi*). Note that the lead hand executes a high section punch at the same time.

Teaching Tip: Bending Ready Stance

You must show full sine wave when moving into this stance so start by dipping lower as the lead leg comes in front of the supporting leg …

… then slightly extend the supporting leg. As you begin to drop into the stance by bending the supporting leg again, start to execute a forearm guarding block.

Complete the stance by dropping sharply into the final position, placing the foot close to the knee with the foot sword parallel to the floor and the knee pointing forwards. Make sure that hands and feet finish moving at the same time.

Won-Hyo

9 Step down with left leg into right I-stance knife hand middle section guarding block (*niunja so sonkal kaunde daebi makgi*).

10 Step forward with right leg and left I-stance knife hand middle section guarding block (*niunja so sonkal kaunde daebi makgi*).

11 Step forward with left leg and right I-stance knife hand middle section guarding block (*niunja so sonkal kaunde daebi makgi*).

Application for Knife Hand Guarding Block: Blocking a Turning Kick

As the attacker starts to execute a turning kick, the defender raises his hands and positions himself to evade the kick …

… and deliver a knife hand guarding block at 45 degrees to the attacker targeting the top of the ankle joint of the kicking leg.

Won-Hyo

12 Step forward into right walking stance middle section straight fingertip thrust (*gunnun so kaunde sun sonkut tulgi*).

13 Turn 270 degrees to the left pivoting on ball of right foot and into right I-stance twin forearm block (*niunja so sang palmok makgi*).

14 Raise body and then drop into right I-stance knife hand high section inward strike (*niunja so sonkal nopunde anuro taerigi*).

Application for 270 degree Turn and Twin Forearm Block: Release from Grab from Side

Defender counter attacks first attacker with straight fingertip thrust as second attacker moves in from behind and to the side …

… and grabs defender strongly by the throat – defender immediately prepares hands and starts to turn to his right …

… and uses increased momentum from 270 degrees turn to execute a strong twin forearm block and release the grab.

Won-Hyo

15 Slip left foot and execute left fixed stance middle section side punch (*gojung so kaunde yop jirugi*).

16 Bring left foot to right, turn 180 degrees to the right pivoting on ball of left foot and into left I-stance twin forearm block (*niunja so sang palmok makgi*).

17 Raise body and then drop into left I-stance knife hand high section inward strike (*niunja so sonkal nopunde anuro taerigi*).

Application for Side Punch: Evade Grab and Counter Attack

As soon as attacker reaches out to grab defender's throat, defender evades by shifting weight to back foot and drawing body up …

… and sliding in to execute side punch in fixed stance to …

… the top of the attacker's rib cage just beneath his armpit.

Won-Hyo

18 Slide right foot and execute right fixed stance middle section side punch (*gojung so kaunde yop jirugi*).

19 Bring right foot to left, turn 90 degrees to the left pivoting on ball of right foot and step forward into left walking stance inner forearm middle section circular block (*gunnun so an palmok kaunde dollimyo makgi*).

20 Keeping hands in the same position deliver right low section front snap kick (*najunde apcha busigi*) …

Teaching Tip: Circular Block

This block must be performed as a single flowing movement clearly showing that you drop underneath the blocking target. Begin with hands held slightly away from the body …

… then bend the front leg so that the knee of the back leg is only inches from the floor; at the same time cross the arms in front of the chest with palms facing downwards and the blocking arm underneath.

Raise body back to the correct height for the stance while executing an inner forearm block. Note that the shoulder of the blocking arm is further forward and slightly lower than that of the reaction arm.

69

Won-Hyo

21 … landing in right walking stance, coming up on the ball of the left foot and extending right arm then forcing heel down to execute right walking stance middle section reverse punch (*gunnun so kaunde bandae jirugi*).

22 Maintaining the same stance, execute right walking stance inner forearm middle section circular block (*gunnun so an palmok kaunde dollimyo makgi*).

23 Keeping hands in the same position deliver left low section front snap kick (*najunde apcha busigi*) …

Application for Circular Block: Blocking Front Snap Kick

As attacker starts to deliver a front snap kick, defender crosses hands and drops body low before …

… rising and executing circular block, catching the attacker's leg and …

… turning attacker so that he lands facing away from defender in a poor position to launch another attack.

Won-Hyo

24 … landing in left walking stance and then executing left walking stance middle section reverse punch (*gunnun so kaunde bandae jirugi*).

25 bring right leg up into left bending ready stance (*guburyo junbi sogi*).

26 Execute right middle section side piercing kick (*kaunde yopcha jirugi*).

Application for Bending Ready Stance and Side Kick: Block and Counter Front Snap Kick

As attacker starts to execute front snap kick, defender raises arms and body and prepares to block kick …

… by dropping sharply into bending ready stance and blocking the kick with the foot sword of the raised leg …

… and then counter attacking immediately with a side kick.

Won-Hyo

27 After kick place right foot next to left, turn 270 degrees to left pivoting on ball of right foot and step into right I-stance forearm middle section guarding block (*niunja so palmok kaunde daebi makgi*).

28 Bring the left foot to the right, turn 180 degrees to the right and step into left I-stance forearm middle section guarding block (*niunja so palmok kaunde daebi makgi*), shout '*kihap*' and then 'Won-Hyo'.

Step back with right leg and return to ready posture: close ready stance A (*moa junbi sogi A*).

Application for 180-degree Turn and Forearm Guarding Block: Counter Attack Against Rush from Behind

Defender hears attacker is running towards him and is almost upon him – defender wants to use attacker's momentum against him so he turns and advances towards him by raising his hands and pulling his lead leg back towards his rear leg …

… and strongly and rapidly advancing towards attacker with twin forearm guarding block. The speed of the technique combined with the motion of the attacker can result in an effective 'blind' checking attack as above …

… or it creates an opportunity to block an attack such as a hooking punch with maximum power and surprise.

7 Yul-Gok Tul

Yul-Gok

Meaning
Yul-Gok is the pseudonym of the great philosopher and scholar Yi I (1536–1584), nicknamed the 'Confucius of Korea'. The thirty-eight movements of this pattern refer to his birthplace on the 38th degree latitude and the diagram of the pattern represents 'scholar'.

Description
The range of blocking and attacking tools continues to be extended in Yul-Gok to include the palm, double forearm and front elbow in this flowing pattern that, like Do-San, pursues moves at angles to the main path of the pattern. With the palm hooking block, the first 'soft' blocking technique is introduced where the purpose is not to block forcefully but to use accuracy and timing to grab the opponent's attacking tool. Timing is also a key element of the first technique in the patterns that uses a jump to close distance before executing a back fist strike in x-stance: here you must not only ensure that that the jump and strike finish at the same time but you must also retain your balance, using the front foot to 'brake' the stance against the momentum of the jump.

There are thirty-eight moves in the pattern and its diagram is:

Grading Syllabus
Yul-Gok is taught at 5th Gup and forms part of the grading examination for 4th Gup that is represented by a blue belt. Blue signifies the Heaven towards which the plant matures into a towering tree as training in Taekwon-Do progresses.

Techniques Introduced

Stances
- x-stance (*kyocha sogi*)

Defensive
- palm middle section hooking block (*sonbadak kaunde golcho makgi*)
- twin knife hand block (*sang sonkal makgi*)
- double forearm high section block (*doo palmok nopunde makgi*)

Offensive
- front elbow strike (*ap palkup taerigi*)

Yul-Gok

Ready posture: parallel ready stance (*narani junbi sogi*).

1 Move left foot in an arc and drop into sitting stance (*annun sogi*) and, at the same time, extending the left arm straight out at shoulder level.

2 Raise body without fully straightening legs and drop down into sitting stance middle section punch (*annun so kaunde ap jirugi*) with the right hand.

Applications for Arm Extension in Sitting Stance: Measure of Distance/Block of Punch

The primary purpose of the initial extension of the arm is to measure up for a punch – in this example, the defender has pushed the attacker back slightly so that he is at the correct distance for a punch to the solar plexus.

Here the movement is used to block a punch from an attacker who is also in sitting stance and at close quarters – the punch is diverted along the outside of the extended arm.

Yul-Gok

3 Slightly dip body then raise without fully straightening legs and drop down into sitting stance middle section punch (*annun so kaunde ap jirugi*) with the left hand. Moves 2 and 3 are performed as a fast motion.

Move left foot to right foot in an arc allowing left arm to bend slightly and extending right arm and crossing on top of left at the wrists.

4 Move right foot in an arc and drop into sitting stance (*annun sogi*) and, at the same time, extending the right arm straight out at shoulder level.

Application for Sitting Stance and Punch: Avoid Punch and Counter Attack to Front

Sitting stance can allow the defender to avoid a technique by moving laterally such as above where the attacker starts to step forward and punch with the right and the defender extends his left arm, dips his body and moves into …

… sitting stance and rapidly counter attacking by punching with the right to the attacker's middle section. Such an application is particularly effective at close quarters and when the defender has only limited room to manoeuvre.

Yul-Gok

5 Raise body without fully straightening legs and drop down into sitting stance middle section punch (*annun so kaunde ap jirugi*) with the left hand.

6 Slightly dip body then raise without fully straightening legs and drop down into sitting stance middle section punch (*annun so kaunde ap jirugi*) with the left hand. Moves 5 and 6 are performed as a fast motion.

7 Move right leg towards left, cross arms and then step forward with right at 45 degrees into right walking stance inner forearm middle section block (*gunnun so an palmok kaunde makgi*).

Application for Sitting Stance and Punch: Avoid Punch and Counter Attack to Side

A variation on the first application is for the defender to avoid the attacker's punch by extending his left arm, dipping his body and stepping into …

… sitting stance at 45 degrees and counter attacking with a right punch to attacker's chest.

Yul-Gok

8 Keep the arms in place and counter attack with left low section front snap kick (*najunde apcha busigi*).

9 After preparing to punch by extending the right arm, step forward raising right heel with left walking stance middle section punch (*gunnun so kaunde ap jirugi*).

10 Force the heel down as you deliver left walking stance middle section reverse punch (*gunnun so kaunde bandae jirugi*). Moves 9 and 10 are performed as a fast motion.

Applications for Low Front Snap Kick and Middle Section Punch: Draw the Head Forward/Make Opponent Drop Guard

Defender counter attacks with a low front snap kick which causes the attacker to start to double up, drawing his head forward...

... and allowing the defender to step down with a punch to the head.

The low front snap kick can also be used as a dummy to draw the opponent's guard down and leave the solar plexus open to the same punch.

Yul-Gok

11 Move left leg towards right, pivoting on ball of right foot to turn 90 degrees to the right and step forward with left leg into left walking stance inner forearm middle section block (*gunnun so an palmok kaunde makgi*).

12 Keep the arms in place and counter attack with right low section front snap kick (*najunde apcha busigi*).

13 After preparing to punch by extending the left arm, step forward raising left heel with right walking stance middle section punch (*gunnun so kaunde ap jirugi*).

Application for Inner Forearm Block and Front Snap Kick: Release from Grab and Counter Attack

As attacker starts to step forward to grab defender's lapel, defender crosses arms, steps back and …

… blocks attacker's grab with inner forearm block to the attacker's inner forearm and counters sharply with …

… low front snap kick to the attacker's groin.

Yul-Gok

14 Force the heel down as you deliver right walking stance middle section reverse punch (*gunnun so kaunde bandae jirugi*). Moves 13 and 14 are performed as a fast motion.

After moving left foot towards right, crossing right hand over left back to back and turn 45 degrees to the right, as you start to block notice that the right hand starts to open out as you raise it …

15 … and step into right walking stance palm middle section hooking block (*gunnun so sonbadak kaunde golcho makgi*) with the right palm. Note that this is a soft technique intended to grab rather than deflect the attacking tool.

Application for Palm Hooking Block: Pulling Attacker Down onto Counter Attack

Defender blocks attacker's punch with a palm hooking block to attacker's inner forearm grabbing the forearm …

… and pulling the opponent forwards and downwards …

… onto a knee strike counter attack to the attacker's middle section.

Yul-Gok

16 Raise the body by coming up on the ball of the left foot and execute right walking stance palm middle section hooking block (*gunnun so sonbadak kaunde golcho makgi*) with the left palm …

17 … and force the heel down as you deliver right walking stance middle section punch (*gunnun so kaunde ap jirugi*). Moves 16 and 17 are performed as a connecting motion (i.e. one breath and one sine wave).

18 Step forward with left leg into left walking stance palm middle section hooking block (*gunnun so sonbadak kaunde golcho makgi*) with the left palm.

Application for Palm Hooking Block: Twisting Attacker's Arm

Here the defender blocks the attacker's punch with a reverse palm hooking block to the attacker's outer wrist …

… grabbing the wrist and …

… sharply pulling the wrist forward parallel to the floor and twisting counter-clockwise at the same to attack opponent's shoulder joint.

80

Yul-Gok

19 Raise the body by coming up on the ball of the right foot and execute left walking stance palm middle section hooking block (*gunnun so sonbadak kaunde golcho makgi*) with the right palm …

20 … and force the heel down as you deliver left walking stance middle section punch (*gunnun so kaunde ap jirugi*). Moves 19 and 20 are performed as a connecting motion.

21 Step forward into right walking stance middle section punch (*gunnun so kaunde ap jirugi*).

Application for Palm Hooking Block: Pulling Attacker Forwards onto Counter Attack

Defender blocks attacker's punch with a reverse palm hooking block to attacker's inner wrist, grabs the wrist …

… and immediately pulls the attacker straight onto a right punch.

Yul-Gok

22 Raise left leg into right bending ready stance (*guburyo sogi*).

23 Execute left middle section side piercing kick (*kaunde yopcha jirugi*) …

24 … and step down with left leg into left left walking stance front elbow strike (*gunnun so ap palkup taerigi*) with the right elbow striking the left palm.

Application for Front Elbow Strike: Pulling Opponent onto Strike

Defender prepares for counter attack by grabbing the attacker around the back of the head and …

… pulling the attacker down onto a front elbow strike aiming at the bridge of the nose.

By grabbing the attacker around the upper back, the technique can also be applied to the upper chest.

Yul-Gok

25 Draw right leg up, turning 180 degrees to the right on the ball of the left foot to execute left bending ready stance (*guburyo sogi*).

26 Execute right middle section side piercing kick (*kaunde yopcha jirugi*) …

27 … and step down with right leg into right walking stance front elbow strike (*gunnun so ap palkup taerigi*) with the left elbow striking the right palm.

Application for Bending Ready Stance and Side Kick: Avoid Sweep and Counter Attack

After counter attacking with front elbow strike, a second attacker moves in to sweep defender's rear leg.

Defender turns and withdraws into bending ready stance to avoid the sweep …

… and counter attacks with a side kick.

Yul-Gok

28 Bring left foot parallel to right, turn body 90 degrees to the left and step forward with left leg into right I-stance twin knife hand block (*sang sonkal makgi*).

29 Step forward into right walking stance straight fingertip thrust (*gunnun so sun sonkut tulgi*).

30 Draw left foot to right, turn 180 degrees to the right pivoting on the ball of the left foot and step forward with right leg left I-stance twin knife hand block (*sang sonkal makgi*).

Application for Twin Knife Hand Block: Defence and Counter Attack against High Hooking Punch

As attacker prepares to throw a high section hooking punch, defender raises hands and ...

... executes twin knife hand block, blocking hooking punch with rising block and simultaneously ...

... counter attacking with knife hand strike to attacker's collar bone. Note that the target is higher because the attacking tool is higher than in the similar application in Dan-Gun.

Yul-Gok

31 Step forward into left walking stance straight fingertip thrust (*gunnun so sun sonkut tulgi*).

32 Turn 90 degrees to the left pivoting on the ball of the right foot and stepping forward with the left leg into left walking stance outer forearm high section side block (*gunnun so bakat palmok nopunde yop makgi*).

33 Raise the body by coming up on the ball of the right foot and then force the heel down into left walking stance middle section reverse punch (*gunnun so kaunde bandae jirugi*).

Application for Straight Fingertip Thrust: Release from Grab and Counter Attack

Attacker grabs defender by the lapel and defender raises hands …

… and attacks grabbing arm with reaction hand whilst simultaneously delivering a straight fingertip thrust to attacker's windpipe.

Yul-Gok

34 Step forward with right walking stance outer forearm high section side block (*gunnun so bakat palmok nopunde yop makgi*).

35 Raise the body by coming up on the ball of the left foot and then force the heel down into right walking stance middle section reverse punch (*gunnun so kaunde bandae jirugi*).

36 Jump back to starting mark landing with left x-stance back fist high section side strike (*kyocha so dung joomuk nopunde yop taerigi*). Note that the right foot is behind the left with the heel slightly raised.

Teaching Tip: Jumping Back Fist Side Strike

The target for the attack is the opponent's temple.

Prepare for the technique by crossing arms in front of chest with attacking arm underneath and heel of rear leg (here the right leg) raises as you start to jump by …

… stepping forward with left leg whilst jumping off the right leg and turning the body into a side facing posture. Jump as low as possible to achieve the required distance (i.e. back to start point).

It is most important that you finish the strike, the withdrawal of the reaction hand to the hip, the placement of the rear foot behind front foot and the dipping of the body by bending both knees all at the same time.

Yul-Gok

37 Turn 180 degrees to the right and step forward with right leg into right walking stance double forearm high section block (*gunnun so doo palmok nopunde makgi*).

38 Bring right foot to left, turn 180 degrees to the left and step forward with left leg into left walking stance double forearm high section block (*gunnun so doo palmok nopunde makgi*), shout '*kihap*' and then 'Yul-Gok'.

Step back with left leg and return to ready posture: parallel ready stance (*narani junbi sogi*).

Application for Double Forearm Block: Defence against Reverse Turning Kick

As attacker prepares to deliver a reverse turning kick, defender raises arms to the side …

… and swings and twists them to forcefully block this strong attack targeting the attacker's Achilles tendon.

Joong-Gun

3 … step forward with right leg into left rear foot stance palm upward block (*dwitbal so sonbadak ollyo makgi*) with the right hand.

4 Bring right foot to left foot turning 180 degrees to the right on the ball of the left foot and step forward with the right foot into left I-stance reverse knife hand middle section side block (*niunja so sonkal dung kaunde yop makgi*).

5 Without moving hands, execute right low section side front snap kick (*najunde yopapcha busigi*). After stepping down with the right leg …

Application for Palm Upward Block: Attack to Head after a Kick

Following on from the previous application, the attacker doubles up after the side front snap kick, lowering his head …

… and defender can step in and strike the head with a palm upward block targeting the nose area. Note that the rear foot stance allows the defender to close the short distance needed to make an effective attack.

Joong-Gun

6 … step forward with left leg into right rear foot stance palm upward block (*dwitbal so sonbadak ollyo makgi*) with the left hand.

7 Turn 90 degrees to the left pivoting on ball of right foot into right I-stance knife hand middle section guarding block (*niunja so sonkal kaunde daebi makgi*).

8 Move left leg into left walking stance upper elbow strike (*gunnun so wi palkup taerigi*).

Application for Palm Upward Block: Blocking a Punch

The more usual application for the palm upward block is against middle section attacks such as above where the attacker steps in with a middle section stepping punch as the defender steps back and starts to move his blocking palm in a circular motion …

… to deliver a palm upward block to the underside of the attacker's arm. The block should 'spring up' the attacker's arm …

… and should target the radial nerve.

Joong-Gun

9 Step forward with right leg into left I-stance knife hand middle section guarding block (*niunja so sonkal kaunde daebi makgi*).

10 Move right leg into right walking stance upper elbow strike (*gunnun so wi palkup taerigi*).

11 Step forward with left leg into left walking stance high section twin vertical punch (*gunnun so nopunde sang sewo jirugi*).

Application for Upper Elbow Strike: Close Quarters Counter Attack

Having defended with a guarding block against a punch, the defender starts to slip his leading foot forward to slide outside attacker's leading leg whilst pulling his rear elbow back in preparation for …

… delivering a rapid and strong counter attack at close quarters with an upper elbow strike to underneath the attacker's chin.

Joong-Gun

12 Step forwards with right leg into right walking stance twin upset punch (*gunnun so sang dwijibo jirugi*).

Move right foot half a shoulder width to the left and execute spot turn 180 degrees to the left, crossing left hand over right as they rise up from waist level …

13 … and you step forward with the left leg into left walking stance x-fist rising block (*gunnun so kyocha joomuk chookyo makgi*).

Teaching Tip: Twin Upset Punch

This close range attack generates its power from a circular motion of the fists. Prepare to step forward by moving the elbows slightly forward of the body with the knuckles upwards and the arms parallel to the floor.

As you step forward pull the fists back and down to the hips as you start to rotate the fists. Keep the elbows close to the body – if you let them move away from the body the technique will lose power.

Make sure that you finish extending the arms and twisting the fists at the same time as you finish stepping.

Note that at completion the elbows are about 5cm from the body with the back fist held slightly higher than the elbow – if the elbows are touching the body you will not have sufficient range to hit the target.

Joong-Gun

14 Move left leg towards right and turn 90 degrees to the left pivoting on the right foot and step with left leg into right I-stance back fist high section side strike with the left hand (*niunja so dung joomuk nopunde yop taerigi*).

15 Twist back fist towards floor in a releasing motion while moving left foot out into left walking stance (*gunnun sogi*).

16 Raise body by coming up on the ball of the right foot and then forcing the right heel down as you execute left walking stance high section reverse punch (*gunnun so nopunde bandae jirugi*). Moves 15 and 16 are performed as a fast motion.

Application for Release and Reverse Punch: Release from Grab and Counter

Defender has his wrist grabbed by attacker after attempting a back fist side strike counter attack. Defender starts to turn the grabbed wrist …

… whilst pulling it sharply downwards (not towards him) and slipping the lead leg into walking stance, releasing the wrist and drawing the attacker down …

… onto a strong reverse punch to the head.

Joong-Gun

17 Move left foot to right foot, turn 180 degrees to the right and step forward with the right leg into left I-stance back fist high section side strike with the right hand (*niunja so dung joomuk nopunde yop taerigi*).

18 Twist back fist towards floor in a releasing motion while moving right foot out into right walking stance (*gunnun sogi*).

19 Raise body by coming up on the ball of the left foot and then forcing the left heel down as you execute right walking stance high section reverse punch (*gunnun so nopunde bandae jirugi*). Moves 18 and 19 are performed as a fast motion.

Application for Release: Release from Grab and Blocking Knee Kick

This release can also be an effective block/strike as shown above where the attacker has grabbed the defender's wrist in order to pull him onto a knee kick.

Defender uses the release from the grab to block the knee kick with …

… a back fist strike to just above the attacker's knee joint.

Joong-Gun

20 Move right foot to left foot, turn 90 degrees to the left, pivoting on ball of right foot and step forward with the left foot into left walking stance double forearm high section block (*gunnun so doo palmok nopunde makgi*).

21 Draw back the left foot and then move it forward into right I-stance middle section side punch (*niunja so kaunde yop jirugi*) with the left fist.

22 Pivoting on the ball of the left foot, deliver a middle section side piercing kick (*kaunde yopcha jirugi*) with the right foot ...

Application for Side Piercing Kick: Defence Against Rushing Attack

Correctly timed, the side piercing kick can be a devastating technique particularly when, as above, an attacker is rushing in. If the defender is some distance away, it is important that he avoids telegraphing his defence and waits until the last moment ...

... before rapidly raising his leg and ...

... delivering a middle section side piercing kick using the attacker's forward momentum to increase the power of the kick.

Joong-Gun

23 ... landing in right walking stance double forearm high section block (*gunnun so doo palmok nopunde makgi*).

24 Draw back the right foot and and then move it forward into left I-stance middle section side punch (*niunja so kaunde yop jirugi*) with the right fist.

25 Pivoting on the ball of the right foot, deliver a middle section side piercing kick (*kaunde yopcha jirugi*) with the left foot ...

Application for Side Punch and Side Piercing Kick: Combination Counter Attack

Unless otherwise stated, middle section side piercing kick is always performed with a high section side punch making it difficult for the opponent to block two simultaneous attacks at different heights.

A useful variation on this combination is to deliver the side punch first causing the attacker to move back ...

... allowing the defender to close the distance quickly and continue to press the attack with a side piercing kick.

Joong-Gun

26 … landing in right I-stance forearm middle section guarding block (*niunja so palmok kaunde daebi makgi*).

Draw left foot back enough to raise the body slightly and as you do so move leading arm down and and rear arm up so that both are parallel to floor at solar plexus height whilst opening the hands …

27 … stepping forward with the left foot, turning the hands over and executing left low stance palm pressing block (*nachuo so sonbadak noollo makgi*) with the right palm. Perform the preparation and the block as a slow motion.

Application for Palm Pressing Block: Blocking Simultaneous Attacks

One attacker starts to deliver front snap kick and another attacker prepares to punch at the same time. Defender extends hands and begins to step in …

… and blocks the front snap kick with the palm pressing block whilst using the reaction hand to deliver a palm upward block to defend against the punch.

Joong-Gun

28 Step forward with the right leg into left I-stance forearm middle section guarding block (*niunja so palmok kaunde daebi makgi*).

29 Draw the right foot back and then step forwards with the right foot into right low stance palm pressing block (*nachuo so sonbadak noollo makgi*) with the left palm. Perform this move as a slow motion.

30 Move left foot to right turning 90 degrees to the left coming up on the balls of the feet and executing close stance angle punch (*moa so giokja jirugi*) as you lower the heels to the floor. Perform this move as a slow motion.

Application for Angle Punch: Turning Opponent onto Punch to Side of Head

Defender blocks a hooking punch with a reverse outer forearm block and grabs attacker's upper punching arm, pulling attacker towards him and turning him at the same time in order to …

… deliver an angle punch to the side of the attacker's head.

Joong-Gun

31 Step forward with right leg into right fixed stance u-shape block (*gojung so digutja makgi*).

32 Move right foot to left foot, step forward with left leg into left fixed stance u-shape block (*gojung so digutja makgi*), shout '*kihap*' and then 'Joong-Gun'.

Step back with left leg and return to ready posture: close ready stance B (*moa junbi sogi B*).

Applications for U-Shape Block: Blocking a Stick/Simultaneous Attack

The standard application for the u-shape block is to defend against a pushing attack with a stick or bayonet. Note that the top blocking arm hands must be held in a vertical line with the upper hand clear of the head and the lower elbow flush with the hip.

The technique can also be used to deliver a simultaneous thrusting attack to the groin and the throat using the arc hand as the attacking tool.

9 Toi-Gye Tul

Toi-Gye

Meaning

Toi-Gye is the pen name of the noted scholar Yi Hwang (sixteenth century), an authority on neo-Confucianism. The thirty-seven movements of this pattern refer to his birthplace on the 37th degree latitude and the diagram of the pattern represents 'scholar'.

Description

Toi-Gye continues to extend the range of Tae-kwon-Do techniques learnt so far by introducing a further thrust and pressing block along with the first pushing block and knee strike. However, its most obvious distinguishing characteristic is its two long sequences of blocking moves that can pose difficulties for students.

Firstly, moves 16 to 21 comprise six consecutive w-shaped blocks, a technique that can look awkward and contrived if not performed correctly and any errors are highlighted when performing this many. Not only must your technique be good in itself but you must also focus strongly in order

to make the last block as sharp and correct as the first.

Secondly, moves 34 to 36 require you to pivot on the balls of both feet to change direction and execute circular blocks – since you are not stepping you must pay particular attention to correctly generating sine wave by bending the rear leg and pushing the hip out.

There are thirty-seven moves in the pattern and its diagram is:

Grading Syllabus

Toi-Gye is taught at 3rd Gup and forms part of the grading examination for 2nd Gup that is represented by a red belt. Red signifies danger, cautioning the student to exercise control and warning the opponent to stay away.

Techniques Introduced

Defensive
- w-shape block (*san makgi*)
- double forearm low section pushing block (*doo palmok najunde miro makgi*)
- x-fist pressing block (*kyocha joomuk noollo makgi*)
- knife hand low section guarding block (*sonkal najunde daebi makgi*)

Offensive
- upset fingertip thrust (*dwijibun sonkut tulgi*)
- back fist side back strike (*dung joomuk yopdwi taerigi*)
- twin side elbow thrust (*sang yop palkup tulgi*)
- knee upward kick (*moorup ollyo chagi*)
- flat fingertip high section thrust (*opun sonkut nopunde tulgi*)

Toi-Gye

Ready posture: close ready stance B (*moa junbi sogi B*).

1 Dip body, look left, raise hands with left hand underneath and palms facing down; turn 90 degrees and step with left foot into right I-stance inner forearm middle section block (*niunja so an palmok kaunde makgi*).

2 Extend left arm, pull back right fist to head height with palm outwards and slip forward with left foot into left walking stance upset fingertip thrust (*gunnun so dwijibun sonkut tulgi*).

Application for Inner Forearm Block and Upset Fingertip Thrust: Blocking a Punch and Counter Attack to the Groin

Attacker steps in with a punch which defender blocks with I-stance inner forearm block …

… then uses hand of blocking arm to grab attacker's punching arm and …

… pulls him onto upset fingertip thrust counter attack to the groin.

Toi-Gye

Bring left foot to right foot coming up on the balls of the feet, turning 90 degrees to the right and crossing arms at chest height with palms facing upwards and the right arm underneath in preparation for ...

3 ... close stance back fist side back strike (*moa so dung joomuk yopdwi taerigi*) with the right hand, lowering the left arm down to the side and the heels to the floor. Perform the preparation and the strike as a slow motion.

4 Turn 90 degrees to the right and step forward with the right leg into left I-stance inner forearm middle section block (*niunja so an palmok kaunde makgi*).

Application for Back Fist Side Back Strike and Low Block: Defence Against Two Close Attackers

As the first attacker prepares to throw a front snap kick the second attacker closes in on defender from behind, defender cannot step back (second attacker is too close) so he crosses arms and ...

... strikes attacker from behind with back fist side back strike and uses reaction arm to block front snap kick from front with low outer forearm block.

Toi-Gye

5 Extend right arm, pull back left fist to head height with palm outwards and slip forward with right foot into right walking stance upset fingertip thrust (*gunnun so dwijibun sonkut tulgi*).

6 Bring right foot to left foot coming up on the balls of the feet and drop down into close stance back fist side back strike (*moa so dung joomuk*) with the left hand, lowering the right arm ro the side Perform this move as a slow motion.

7 Step forward with left leg into left walking stance x-fist pressing block (*gunnun so kyocha joomuk noollo makgi*).

Application for Upset Finger Thrust: Counter Attack to the Scrotum

Having blocked a punch, defender counter attacks by executing an upset fingertip thrust to the genital area and grabbing attacker's scrotum …

… then using the back fist side back strike movement to pull attacker's scrotum sharply.

Toi-Gye

Raise body by coming up on the ball of the right foot and draw hands back towards chest with palms facing inwards …

8 … and drop body down into left walking stance high section twin vertical punch (*gunnun so nopunde sang sewo jirugi*). Perform moves 7 and 8 as a continuous motion.

9 Keeping the hands in the same position, execute a middle section front snap kick (*kaunde apcha busigi*) with the right leg.

Application for X-Fist Pressing Block and Twin Vertical Punch: Blocking a Front Snap Kick and Counter Attack to Face

Having blocked a front snap kick with a two handed x-fist pressing block, the defender is well placed to deliver …

… a two handed counter attack like this twin vertical punch targeting the cheek bones.

Toi-Gye

10 After preparing to punch by extending the left arm, step down with right leg into right walking stance middle section punch (*gunnun so kaunde ap jirugi*).

11 Raise body by coming up on the ball of the left foot and drop down into right walking stance middle section reverse punch (*gunnun so kaunde bandae jirugi*) with the left fist.

12 Bring left foot to right foot, turning 90 degrees to the left, coming up on the balls of the feet with arms in position and dropping down into close stance twin side elbow thrust (*moa so sang yop palkup tulgi*). Perform this move as a slow motion.

Application for Twin Elbow Thrust: Release from Shoulder Grab

As soon as attacker grabs defender by the shoulders from the front …

… defender immediately takes a step back turning to the side …

… and delivering elbow thrust as grip is broken.

Toi-Gye

13 Turning 90 degrees to the left on the ball of the left foot, raise the right leg and stamp down into sitting stance w-shape block (*annun so san makgi*) with the right forearm and looking to the right.

14 Turning 180 degrees to the right on the ball of the right foot, raise the left leg and stamp down into sitting stance w-shape block (*annun so san makgi*) with the left forearm and looking to the left.

15 Turning 180 degrees to the right on the ball of the right foot, raise the left leg and stamp down into sitting stance w-shape block (*annun so san makgi*) with the left forearm and looking to the left.

Teaching Tip: W-Shape Block

Start the block with the arms forming a w-shape with elbows held slightly lower than the shoulder. As you raise the leg on the blocking side, twist the forearms in that direction.

Fully raise the leg on the blocking side so that the thigh is parallel to the floor whilst pivoting on the ball of the supporting leg. Twist the trunk so that the upper body 'follows' the legs.

Finish the block by twisting the forearms and the trunk at the last moment to deliver maximum power to the blocking forearm as you land into sitting stance.

Toi-Gye

16 Turning 180 degrees to the left on the ball of the left foot, raise the right leg and stamp down into sitting stance w-shape block (*annun so san makgi*) with the right forearm and looking to the right.

17 Turning 180 degrees to the right on the ball of the right foot, raise the left leg and stamp down into sitting stance w-shape block (*annun so san makgi*) with the left forearm and looking to the left.

18 Turning 180 degrees to the right on the ball of the right foot, raise the left leg and stamp down into sitting stance w-shape block (*annun so san makgi*) with the left forearm and looking to the left.

Applications for W-Shape Block: Blocking a Kick/Punch

This block is used against high section attacks such as this high section reverse turning kick.

Where the attacker's foot is in range such as when blocking against a high section stepping punch the defender can use the blocking motion to stamp on the attacker's foot.

Toi-Gye

Move right foot to left foot, turn 90 degrees to the right, pivoting on the ball of the right foot, raising both hands to shoulder height with the palms facing outwards …

19 … stepping forward with the left leg into right I-stance double forearm low section pushing block (*niunja so doo palmok najunde miro makgi*).

20 Move left foot out into left walking stance, extending both arms as though grabbing attacker's head …

Application for Double Forearm Pushing Block:
Blocking a Front Snap Kick and Forcing Attacker off Balance

Attacker executes a front snap kick and defender blocks with double forearm pushing block not only to block the attack but also to …

… push the attacker off balance allowing …

… defender to follow up with a grab to the head.

Toi-Gye

21 … pull hands downwards and at the same time execute knee upward kick (*moorup ollyo chagi*) with the right knee. Note that the supporting leg is bent as the kick is delivered.

22 After the kick move right foot to left foot, turn 180 degrees to the left and step forward with the left leg into right I-stance knife hand middle section guarding block (*niunja so sonkal kaunde daebi makgi*).

23 Without moving hands execute a low section side front snap kick (*najunde yopapcha busigi*) with the left leg …

Application for Knee Upward Kick: Close Quarters Kick to Head/Abdomen

Where the head is already lowering (as in the previous application), continue to pull it down and execute the upward knee strike to the face.

At very close quarters, pulling the opponent's head down partially allows you to target the abdominal/lower chest area.

Toi-Gye

24 … landing in left walking stance flat fingertip high section thrust (*gunnun so opun sonkut nopunde tulgi*) with the left hand.

25 Step forward with right leg into left I-stance knife hand middle section guarding block (*niunja so sonkal kaunde daebi makgi*).

26 Without moving hands execute a low section side front snap kick (*najunde yopapcha busigi*) with the right leg …

Application for Flat Fingertip Thrust: Counter Attack to Soft Tissue Targets

The flat fingertip thrust is extremely effective when applied to soft tissue high section targets such as the throat …

… or the eyes. Remember: such targets can never be conditioned and they will always be equally effective against any opponent regardless of size or physical conditioning.

Toi-Gye

27 ... landing in right walking stance flat fingertip high section thrust (*gunnun so opun sonkut nopunde tulgi*) with the right hand.

28 Step backwards with the right leg into right I-stance back fist side back strike (*niunja so dung joomuk yopdwi taerigi*) with the right arm and outer forearm low section block (*bakat palmok najunde makgi*) with the left.

29 Jump forward a full stance length with the legs bent and the feet clear of the ground, landing in right x-stance x-fist pressing block (*kyocha so kyocha joomuk noollo makgi*).

Application for Low Block and Back Fist Side Back Strike: Defence Against Two Attackers

As in the application for moves 3 and 4, as attacker steps in with front snap kick a second attacker closes in from behind but from further back, defender crosses hands and ...

... steps back blocking the front snap kick with a low block and delivering a back fist side back strike to the second attacker.

Toi-Gye

30 Step forward with right leg into right walking stance double forearm high section block (*gunnun so doo palmok nopunde makgi*).

31 Turn 270 degrees to the left pivoting on the ball of the right foot and then step forward with the left leg into right I-stance knife hand low section guarding block (*niunja so sonkal najunde daebi makgi*).

32 Move the left leg into left walking stance inner forearm middle section circular block (*gunnun so an palmok kaunde dollimyo makgi*). Note that the block is at 45 degrees from the direction of the stance.

Application for X-Fist Pressing Block and Double Forearm Block: Blocking Successive Attacks

Defender blocks first attacker's close range front snap kick with x-fist pressing block as the second attacker approaches from the side. Defender use of x-stance allows him rapidly to …

… turn and step into second attacker using double forearm block to strike attacker's neck/jaw.

Toi-Gye

33 Move left foot to right foot turning 180 degrees to the right and step with the right leg into left I-stance knife hand low section guarding block (*niunja so sonkal najunde daebi makgi*).

34 Move the right leg into right walking stance inner forearm middle section circular block (*gunnun so an palmok kaunde dollimyo makgi*). Again, note that the block is at 45 degrees from the direction of the stance.

35 Pivot on the balls of both feet turning 135 degrees to the right and into left walking stance inner forearm middle section circular block (*gunnun so an palmok dollimyo makgi*).

Application for Low Knife Hand Guarding Block and Circular Block: Blocking Two Attackers

As first attacker starts to kick, defender …

… blocks front snap kick with knife hand low section guarding block as second attack steps in from 45 degrees angle with a punch …

… which defender blocks with an angled circular block.

Toi-Gye

36 Pivot on the balls of both feet turning to the right and back to stance held in move 34 executing right walking stance inner forearm middle section circular block (*gunnun so an palmok kaunde dollimyo makgi*), blocking at 45 degrees.

37 Move right foot parallel to left foot turning 90 degrees to the left and into sitting stance middle section punch (*annun so kaunde ap jirugi*) with the right arm, shout 'kihap' and then 'Toi-Gye'.

Step with right leg and return to ready posture: close ready stance B (*moa junbi sogi B*).

Application for Circular Block and Sitting Stance Punch: Blocking and Countering a Turning Kick

Attacker executes a turning kick which defender blocks with a circular block …

… which turns the attacker and …

… allows defender to move into sitting stance and counter with a punch to attacker's kidney.

10   Hwa-Rang Tul

Hwa-Rang

Meaning

Hwa-Rang is named after the Hwa-Rang youth group that originated in the Silla dynasty in the early seventh century. The twenty-nine movements of the pattern refer to the 29th Infantry Division where Taekwon-Do developed into maturity.

Description

Hwa-Rang breaks with the symmetry of the earlier patterns by no longer mirroring moves performed to the left of the starting point by replicating them on the right, preparing the student for the black belt patterns.

This dynamic pattern emphasizes sustained attack opening with a long lateral combination in moves 1 to 8 that pushes the opponent back with successive hand techniques using five different stances and later introducing the first high section kick with the turning kick. Note the use of sliding as well as stance changes to make both large and small adjustments in range to pursue attacks: the student should now be capable of more subtle strategies than merely stepping forwards and backwards – try and use these techniques in your sparring.

There are twenty-nine moves in the pattern and its diagram is:

Grading Syllabus

Hwa-Rang is taught at 2nd Gup and forms part of the grading examination for 1st Gup that is represented by a red belt with a black stripe.

Techniques Introduced

Stances
- close ready stance C (*moa junbi sogi C*)
- vertical stance (*soojik sogi*)

Defensive
- palm middle section pushing block (*sonbadak kaunde miro makgi*)
- inner forearm side front block (*an palmok yopap makgi*)

Offensive
- upward punch (*ollyo jirugi*)
- knife hand downward strike (*sonkal naeryo taerigi*)
- high section turning kick (*nopunde dollyo chagi*)
- side elbow thrust (*yop palkup tulgi*)

Hwa-Rang

Ready posture: close ready stance C (*moa junbi sogi C*).

1 Step sideways with left leg into sitting stance palm middle section pushing block (*annun so sonbadak kaunde miro makgi*) with the left palm.

2 Execute sitting stance middle section front punch (*annun so kaunde ap jirugi*) with the right arm.

Application for Palm Pushing Block and Punch: Blocking a Punch and Counter Attacking

Attacker steps in with a middle section punch and defender avoids by stepping to the side and executing a palm pushing block to the shoulder of the attacking arm which both turns the attacker and forces him off balance …

… allowing defender to counter with a punch to the base of attacker's skull …

Hwa-Rang

3 Execute sitting stance middle section front punch (*annun so kaunde ap jirugi*) with the left arm.

4 Raise the body slightly, turning 90 degrees to the right and move the right foot into left I-stance twin forearm block (*niunja so sang palmok makgi*).

Raise the body slightly and start to describe two large circles with the fists …

Application for Twin Forearm Block and Upward Punch: Blocking a Hook Punch and Counter Attacking

Defender blocks attacker's hook punch with twin forearm block …

… and grabs attacker's head with lead hand, pulling him down onto …

… upward punch striking the attacker's cheek bone.

Hwa-Rang

5 ... dropping the body as the fists complete their circles into left I-stance upward punch (*niunja so ollyo jirugi*) with the left hand – note that the right side fist is placed on the left shoulder.

6 Pushing off the left foot slide into right fixed stance middle section side punch (*gojung so kaunde yop jirugi*).

Raise body and start to draw right foot back extending left reaction arm and starting to move right knife hand in large overhead arc to deliver ...

Application for Sliding Side Punch: Pursuing a Counter Attack

As attacker reels back from the first counter attack, defender slips leading foot back and raises body to close increased distance with ...

... sliding side punch to attacker's middle section.

Hwa-Rang

7 Left vertical stance knife hand downward strike (*soojik so sonkal naeryo taerigi*).

8 Step forward with left leg into left walking stance middle section punch (*gunnun so kaunde ap jirugi*).

9 Move left foot to right foot turn 90 degrees to the left, pivoting on ball of right foot and step forward with left leg into left walking stance outer forearm low section block (*gunnun so bakat palmok najunde makgi*).

Application for Knife Hand Downward Strike: Pursuing a Counter Attack

Where an initial counter attack such as a front snap kick causes attacker to bend forwards at close range …

… defender pursues the counter attack with knife hand downward strike to the trapezius muscle/top of the spine, depending on the angle that the upper body drops.

Hwa-Rang

10 Step forward with right leg into right walking stance middle section punch (*gunnun so kaunde ap jirugi*).

11 Move left foot forward towards right foot covering right fist with left palm and bending right elbow by 45 degrees.

12 Execute middle section side piercing kick (*kaunde yopcha jirugi*) pulling both hands sharply back to the solar plexus …

Application for Grab and Side Kick: Pulling Attacker onto Kick

Attacker evades defender's counter punch and grabs defender's fist.

Defender places his palm over back of attacker's hand grabbing it firmly whilst moving his back leg forwards slightly in order to …

… pull attacker onto side piercing kick.

Hwa-Rang

... stepping down with the right leg in front and into left I-stance knife hand side strike (*niunja so sonkal yop taerigi*).

13 Step forward with left leg into left walking stance middle section punch (*gunnun so kaunde ap jirugi*) with the left fist.

14 Step forward with right leg into right walking stance middle section punch (*gunnun so kaunde ap jirugi*) with the right fist.

Application for Knife Hand Side Strike: Pursuing a Counter Attack

Continuing with the previous application, a strong side kick will cause the attacker to double up and drop his head, probably moving slightly backwards ...

... defender can rapidly pursue his counter attack by executing a knife hand side strike as he lands from the kick targeting the carotid artery in the neck.

Hwa-Rang

15 Turn 270 degrees to the left pivoting on the ball of the right foot and into right I-stance knife hand middle section guarding block (*niunja so sonkal kaunde daebi makgi*).

16 Step forward with the right leg into right walking stance straight fingertip thrust (*gunnun so sun sonkut tulgi*).

17 Move right foot one shoulder width to the left and perform a spot turn turning 180 degrees to the left and into right I-stance knife hand middle section guarding block (*niunja so sonkal kaunde daebi makgi*).

Applications for Turning and Straight Fingertip Thrust: Release from Grab and Counter Attack

Attacker evades defender's counter punch and grabs defender's fist.

Defender turns 270 degrees and executes knife hand guarding block to attacker's elbow to break grab …

… and counters with a straight fingertip thrust to upper rib area just beneath attacker's armpit.

Hwa-Rang

18 Execute a high section turning kick (*nopunde dollyo chagi*) with the right leg landing with the right leg in front and …

19 … execute a high section turning kick (*nopunde dollyo chagi*) with the left leg landing with the left leg in front and into …

… right I-stance knife hand middle section guarding block (*niunja so sonkal kaunde daebi makgi*). Perform moves 18 and 19 as a fast motion.

Teaching Tip: Turning Kick

Start the kick by raising the kicking leg fully flexed and with the hands held in a guarding position.

Pivoting on the ball of the supporting foot, turn the hips until they are in line with the target at 45 degrees from the front, extending the leg as you do so – keep the arms in a guarding position.

After striking the target retract the leg fully before stepping down.

Hwa-Rang

20 Turn 90 degrees to the left pivoting on the ball of the right foot and into left walking stance outer forearm low section block (*gunnun so bakat palmok najunde makgi*).

21 Pull the left foot back slightly and then slip it forward into right I-stance middle section punch (*niunja so kaunde ap jirugi*) with the right fist.

22 Step forward with the right leg into left I-stance middle section punch (*niunja so kaunde ap jirugi*) with the left fist.

Application for Low Block and L-Stance Obverse Punch: Blocking a Knee Kick and Counter Attacking

Defender steps back and blocks attacker's knee kick with outer forearm low section block …

… and drops back into I-stance as attacker falls forward, counter attacking with an obverse punch to the chest.

Hwa-Rang

23 Step forward with the left leg into right I-stance middle section punch (*niunja so kaunde ap jirugi*) with the right fist.

24 Slip the left foot out into left walking stance x-fist pressing block (*gunnun so kyocha joomuk noollo makgi*). Note that the right fist is on top of the left.

Step forward with the right leg turning 180 degrees to the left and cross right arm underneath left as you ...

Application for X-Fist Pressing Block: Blocking a Front Snap Kick

As attacker starts to execute front snap kick, defender raises body and hands in order to ...

... drop down into x-fist pressing block, targeting the front of the ankle joint.

126

Hwa-Rang

25 … slide right foot back to starting point and into right I-stance side elbow thrust (*niunja so yop palkup tulgi*) with the right elbow.

26 Bring left foot to right foot turning 90 degrees to the left into close stance inner forearm side front block (*moa so an palmok yopap makgi*) with the right arm and outer forearm low section block (*bakat palmok najunde makgi*) with the left.

27 Come up on the balls of the feet and then down into close stance inner forearm side front block (*moa so an palmok yopap makgi*) with the left arm and outer forearm low section front block (*bakat palmok najunde makgi*) with the right.

Application for Sliding Elbow Strike: Pursuing a Counter Attack

As attacker reels back from the x-fist pressing block, defender needs to pursue his counter attack by …

… turning and sliding with an elbow strike to the abdomen.

Hwa-Rang

28 Step forward with the left leg into right I-stance knife hand middle section guarding block (*niunja so sonkal kaunde daebi makgi*).

29 Move left foot to right turning 180 degrees to the right and into left I-stance knife hand middle section guarding block (*niunja so sonkal kaunde daebi makgi*), shout 'kihap' and then 'Hwa-Rang'.

Step back with right leg and return to ready posture: close ready stance C (*moa junbi sogi C*).

Applications for 180 degrees Turn and Knife Hand Guarding Block: Defence Against Two Attackers

Knife hand guarding block is not only effective as a block against a variety of attacks such as the first attacker's turning kick above …

… but it can also be a strong attack at close quarters such above where defender turns just as second attacker is almost upon him and counters with knife hand guarding block targeting the collar bone.

11   Choong-Moo Tul

Choong-Moo

Meaning

Choong-Moo was the name given to the great Admiral Yi Soon-Sin of the Yi dynasty who was reputed to have invented the first armoured battleship (*Kobukson*) in 1592 which is said to be the precursor of the present day submarine. The reason why this pattern ends with a left-handed attack is to symbolize his regrettable death: he was never allowed to reach his full potential as he was forced to be loyal to the king.

Description

This spectacular pattern that emphasizes kicking is the last of the coloured belt patterns and introduces some of the hallmark aerial techniques for which Taekwon-Do is renowned. Specifically, we see the first flying kick with the flying side piercing kick and a jumping 360-degree turning knife hand

guarding block both of which must be executed in the air at the highest point of the jump landing with no loss of full balance and in the correct stance.

Choong-Moo therefore not only shows that the student has grasped the fundamentals necessary for gaining a black belt but also points to the challenges ahead as you delve deeper into the art, no longer a beginner but with a great deal yet to learn.

There are thirty moves in the pattern and its diagram is:

Grading Syllabus

Choong-Moo is taught at 1st Gup and forms part of the grading examination for 1st Dan black belt. Black is the opposite of white, the beginner's colour, and therefore signifies maturity and proficiency in Taekwon-Do. It also indicates the wearer's imperviousness to darkness and fear.

Techniques Introduced

Defensive
- inner forearm middle section inner front block (*an palmok kaunde ap makgi*)
- x-knife hand checking block (*kyocha sonkal momchau makgi*)
- twin palm upward block (*sang sonbadak ollyo makgi*)

Offensive
- flying side piercing kick (*twimyo yopcha jirugi*)
- reverse knife hand high section front strike (*sonkal dung nopunde ap taerigi*)
- middle section back piercing kick (*kaunde dwitcha jirugi*)

Choong-Moo

Ready posture: parallel ready stance (*narani junbi sogi*).

1 Dip body, look left raise hands as for twin knife hand block; turn 90 degrees to the left and step with the left leg into right I-stance twin knife hand block (*niunja so sang sonkal makgi*).

As you step forward with the right leg start to raise left hand in front of face and to move the right in a circular motion with palms facing outwards and step into ...

Application for Knife Hand Inward Strike: Counter Attack after Blocking

Defender has blocked a punch ...

... as defender steps forward, he raises his hands which raises the attacker's punching arm and counters with ...

... inward knife hand strike to attacker's neck.

Choong-Moo

2 … right walking stance knife hand high section front strike (*gunnun so sonkal nopunde ap taerigi*) with the right hand and the left hand in front of the forehead, palm facing outwards.

3 Turn 180 degrees to the right pivoting on the ball of the left foot and stepping with the right leg into left I-stance knife hand middle section guarding block (*niunja so sonkal kaunde daebi makgi*).

4 Step forward with the left leg into left walking stance flat fingertip high section thrust (*gunnun so opun sonkut nopunde tulgi*) with the left hand.

Application for Knife Hand Inward Strike: Blocking and Countering an Overhead Strike at the Same Time

Another use of the reaction hand in this technique is as a block against an overhead technique such as stepping into an attempted strike with a weapon …

… and using the reaction hand as a knife hand rising block at the same time as counter attacking with a knife hand high section inward strike to the attacker's neck.

131

Choong-Moo

5 Turn 90 degrees to the left and step with left leg into right I–stance middle section guarding block (*niunja so sonkal kaunde daebi makgi*).

6 Turn 180 degrees to the right pivoting on the ball of the left foot and drawing up the right leg into left bending ready stance (*guburyo sogi*).

7 Execute a middle section side piercing kick (*kaunde yopcha jirugi*) with the right leg lowering the right foot next to the left and …

Application for Knife Hand Guarding Block and Side Kick: Defence against Two Attackers

Defender blocks first attacker's knife attack with knife hand guarding block as second attacker prepares to execute side kick from behind …

… which defender avoids by turning to face second attacker and pulling back into bending ready stance …

… and countering with a side piercing kick.

Choong-Moo

8 … turn 180 degrees to the left pivoting on the ball of the right foot and stepping forward with the left into right I-stance knife hand middle section guarding block (*niunja so sonkal kaunde daebi makgi*).

Step forward with right leg and …

… jump up in the air with the left leg tucked in and the right raised to deliver …

Application for Flying Side Piercing Kick: Closing Distance for Counter Attack

Sometimes it is necessary to close a substantial distance quickly and with the maximum surprise and momentum …

… stepping in with the flying side piercing kick …

… covers two full strides with a single step.

Choong-Moo

9 … flying side piercing kick (*twimyo yopcha jirugi*) with the right leg landing in …

… left I-stance knife hand middle section guarding block (*niunja so sonkal daebi makgi*).

10 Turn 270 degrees to the left pivoting on the ball of the right foot and step forward with the left leg into right I-stance outer forearm low section block (*niunja so bakat palmok najunde makgi*) with the left arm.

Application for Flying Side Piercing Kick: Clearing Obstacle to Pursue Counter Attack

In addition to closing distance, flying kicks are very useful in clearing objects between defender and attacker. In this case defender has dealt with first attacker who falls to the ground in front of the second attacker …

… so defender jumps up to clear fallen first attacker …

… and deliver a flying side piercing kick against the second attacker.

Choong-Moo

11 Move left foot out into left walking stance, extending both arms as though grabbing attacker's head …

12 … pull hands downwards and at the same time execute knee upward kick (*moorup ollyo chagi*) with the right knee.

13 After the kick move right foot to left foot, turn 180 degrees to the left and step forward with left leg into left walking stance reverse knife hand high section front strike (*gunnun so sonkal dung nopunde ap taerigi*) with the right arm.

Application for Reverse Knife Hand Strike: Counter Attack to Temple

In order to deliver maximum power, defender swings his attacking arm in a wide arc while holding it almost straight …

… ideally connecting to the target with a slight downward angle.

Choong-Moo

14 Execute a high section turning kick (*nopunde dollyo chagi*) landing with the right foot next to the left foot …

15 … turning 180 degrees to the right to deliver a middle section back piercing kick (*kaunde dwitcha jirugi*) with the left leg. Moves 14 and 15 are performed as a fast motion.

16 After the kick, lower the left leg behind the right into left I-stance forearm middle section guarding block (*niunja so palmok kaunde daebi makgi*).

Applications for Back Piercing Kick: Defence against Attack from Behind

The back piercing kick is highly effective against an attack from the rear since it combines reach with speed. As attacker steps from behind, defender glances over his shoulder and raises the leg on the same side …

… to deliver back piercing kick to the attacker's solar plexus keeping the toes pointed down and attacking with the heel.

Choong-Moo

17 Execute a middle section turning kick (*kaunde dollyo chagi*) with the left leg.

18 Lower the left foot to the right foot, turn 90 degrees to the right and step forward with the right leg into right fixed stance u-shape block (*gojung so digutja makgi*).

19 Without moving the feet jump straight up, tucking the legs up …

Application for U-Shape Block and Jump: Block Stick and Avoid Sweep

Having had his pushing attack with the stick blocked by a u-shape block, the attacker withdraws the staff …

… and starts to swing at defender's legs …

… as defender jumps to avoid sweep.

Choong-Moo

… turn 360 degrees in the air, landing in …

… left I-stance knife hand middle section guarding block (*niunja so sonkal kaunde daebi makgi*).

20 Step forward with the left leg into left walking stance upset fingertip thrust (*gunnun so dwijibun sonkut tulgi*) with the right arm.

Application for U-Shape Block and Jump Continued: Block Further Attack on Landing

As defender avoids leg sweep by jumping, attacker continues with attack by following through with …

… strike in the opposite direction which defender starts to block in the air …

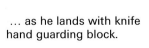

… as he lands with knife hand guarding block.

Choong-Moo

21 Slip the left foot into right I-stance back fist side back strike (*niunja so dung joomuk nopunde yopdwi taerigi*) with the right arm and outer forearm low section block (*bakat palmok najunde makgi*) with the left.

22 Step forward with the right foot into right walking stance straight fingertip thrust (*gunnun so sun sonkut tulgi*) with the right arm.

23 Turn 270 degrees to the left pivoting on the ball of the right foot and step forward with the left leg into left walking stance double forearm high section block (*gunnun so doo palmok nopunde makgi*).

Application for Low Block/Back Fist and Straight Fingertip Thrust: Defence Against Two Attackers

Both attackers close in from in front of and behind the attacker …

… defender blocks first attacker's front snap kick with a low block whilst stopping the second attacker with a high back fist strike and …

… counter attacking the first attacker with straight fingertip thrust.

Choong-Moo

24 Turn 90 degrees to the left pivoting on the ball of the left foot and into sitting stance inner forearm middle section front block (*annun so an palmok kaunde ap makgi*) with the right arm …

… and looking to the right execute a back fist high section side strike (*annun so dung joomuk nopunde yop taerigi*) with the right arm.

25 Turn 90 degrees to the left pivoting on the ball of the left foot and execute a middle section side piercing kick (*kaunde yopcha jirugi*) with the right leg …

Application for Inner Forearm Block and Back Fist: Blocking a Punch and Counter Attack

Defender blocks punch by turning into attack with inner forearm block in sitting stance and …

… counters immediately with a back fist strike using the blocking arm.

140

Choong-Moo

26 … landing with the right foot next to the left and executing a middle section side piercing kick (*kaunde yopcha jirugi*) with the left leg …

27 … landing with the left leg next to the right, turning 180 degrees to the right and stepping with the right leg into left I-stance x-knife hand checking block (*niunja so kyocha sonkal momchau makgi*).

28 Step forward with the left leg into left walking stance twin palm upward block (*gunnun so sang sonbadak ollyo makgi*).

Application for Twin Palm Upward Block: Blocking Twin Upset Punch

Attacker begins to step in to punch with …

… twin upset punch which the defender steps in and blocks with twin palm upward block.

Choong-Moo

  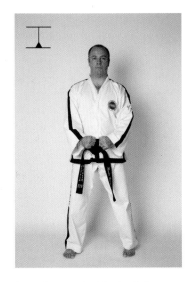

29 Spot turn 180 degrees to the right pivoting on the ball of the left foot and stepping forward with the right leg into right walking stance outer forearm rising block (*gunnun so bakat palmok chookyo makgi*) with the right arm.

30 Extend right arm and execute right walking stance middle section reverse punch (*gunnun so kaunde bandae jirugi*) with the left arm, shout '*kihap*' and then 'Choong-Moo'.

Step forward with the left leg and return to ready posture: parallel ready stance (*narani junbi sogi*).

**Application for Forearm Rising Block and Reverse Punch:
Blocking a Punch and Counter Attack to Throat**

Defender blocks attacker's high section punch with forearm rising block …

… countering immediately with a reverse punch targeting the attacker's throat.

142

Index